CW00542957

For Vera, Louisa and Kerri.

The Warwickshire Aborigine

The Warwickshire Aborigine

Bernie Byrne

LIVE WIRE

Copyright Bernie Byrne 2006

All rights reserved. No part of this publication may
be reproduced or stored in a retrieval system or
transmitted in any form or by any means, electronic,
mechanical, photocopying or otherwise without the
prior written permission of the publisher.

First published in 2006 by

Live Wire Books
The Orchard, School Lane
Warmington, Banbury
Oxfordshire OX17 1DE

Tel: 01295 690358
info@livewirebooks.com
www.livewirebooks.com

The right of Bernie Byrne to be identified as the author
of this work has been asserted in accordance with the
Copyright, Designs and Patents Act 1988.

ISBN 0-9553124-0-X / 978-0-9553124-0-3

A catalogue record for this book is available from the
British Library.

Designed by Dick Malt 01362 860237
Printed and bound in Dubai by Oriental Press

Picture credits

Section 1, page 3 (bottom): Courtesy of JCB
Section 2, page 8 (bottom): Avon Studios,
    Wellesbourne
Section 3, page 5: Courtesy of *The Journal*
Section 3, page 8 (top): Avon Studios, Wellesbourne

Contents

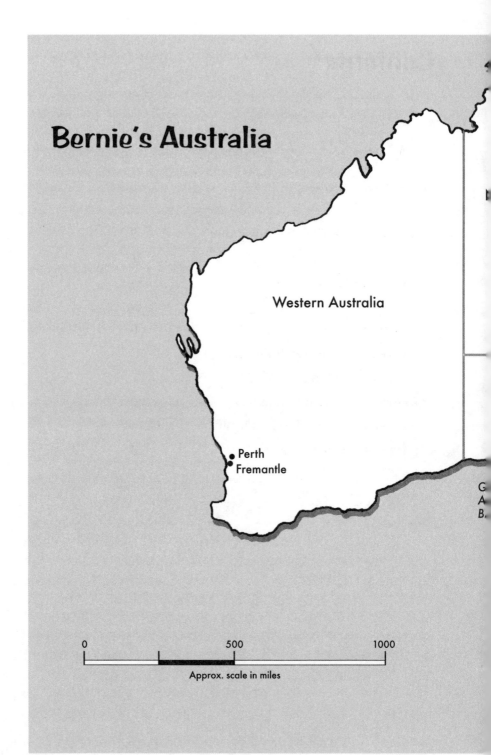

Bernie's Australia

Western Australia

● Perth
● Fremantle

G
A
B.

0   500   1000

Approx. scale in miles

Acknowledgements

I would first like to thank Michael Cable of Live Wire Books, without whose help I might never have had the satisfaction of seeing my scribbled memoirs in print.

I would also like to express my gratitute to Barb, Jon and Jackie for all the love and support that they gave me during that very stressful time after I first returned from Australia and that they have continued to give me ever since. I would like Mum ('Wowey') to know that she will always be 'numero uno'; and to Tiffany I would just like to say – thanks for being my daughter.

Thanks also to Nigel Ridout, for providing Barb and me with a home in which to start our new life together; to Reggie Walker, Barb's brother, for helping me to regain my sense of humour during that difficult period after I first came back to England; to Andrew and Betty Bryan, for their unconditional friendship; to Andrew and John Wrench, for giving me the chance to regain my self-confidence; to Mick Williams, Barb's former husband, for being 100% understanding; to brother Bob, for getting in touch despite all the obstacles; to Phil and Pat, for their invaluable information; and, last but by no means least, to the Shipston Ladies Hockey Team, for whom Jackie plays, for their unconditional friendship and entertainment both on and off the pitch.

CHAPTER 1

A Taste For Adventure

Australia? Why Australia, I asked myself?

It was a Friday night and, as usual, my mate Roy Pool and I were propping up the bar at The Horseshoe Inn, our local pub in Shipston-on-Stour. At the end of another hard week down on the farm we were both feeling thoroughly fed up with our lot. Stuck in a rut, broke most of the time and with no great future ahead of us as far as we could see, we were desperate to break away and start a new life.

We first thought about joining the Merchant Navy, but when we made inquiries we were told that the only jobs available to a couple of landlubbers like us would be as galley slaves or lowly engine room ratings. Peeling spuds or sweating away as oily rags in the steam heat down below decks didn't sound very exciting so we decided to give that a miss. Next, we toyed with the idea of becoming mercenaries in Africa with 'Mad Mike' Hoare, only to discover that although the money was very good, the average life expectancy was about six weeks. That seemed a bit too exciting!

It was then that we came across a newspaper advert offering 'assisted passage' to Australia for a price of just £10 for anyone wanting to emigrate there from the UK. Post-war Australian governments were desperate to boost the workforce in their under-populated country and more than a million Brits – the so-called '£10 Poms' – went over between the late 1940s and the mid-seventies, lured by the promise of wonderful new opportunities in a land of milk and honey.

Over pints of the cheapest 'cooking' bitter, which, at 1/10d-a-pint (less than 10p), was all we could afford at the time, Roy and I sat in

The Horseshoe that night in 1965 and talked it over. I had a few misgivings at first about making quite such a drastic move, but Roy had already made up his mind to go and after thinking it over for a couple of days, I agreed to join him.

Everybody else thought we'd both gone stark raving mad. After all, it really was the other side of the world in those days. But the way we looked at it – what had we got to lose? We might possibly make our fortunes. And if things didn't quite work out we could always come back after a couple of years and boast about our adventures. It's true that Roy had a steady girlfriend at the time – she was to remain blissfully unaware of his plans until just a few days before we left! – but as far as I was concerned, there was absolutely nothing to hold me back.

Except, that is, for one minor problem. I was still only twenty years old at the time – a couple of years younger than Roy – and having just fallen out for good with my father, with whom I had always had an extremely strained relationship, I knew there was no way I would ever be able to get him to sign the necessary papers on my behalf. As a result, we had to wait a few more months, until I was twenty-one, before we could go ahead with our applications.

On the very day of my twenty-first birthday, we sent off the completed forms. Then, once all the paperwork had been completed, we had to go along for a medical. The only hiccup here came when we were asked to provide a urine sample. Despite the fact that we'd spent about three hours in the pub beforehand, we found it difficult to produce on demand. Turning the taps on in the loo eventually did the trick and although the resulting specimens must have been about 50% IPA bitter, we were passed A1 and accepted for immigration.

The deal was simple. You paid £10 towards your travelling expenses – and that was it. The Australian government picked up the bill for everything else, including all your meals on the ship going over; they even paid our rail fares from Birmingham down to Southampton.

There was one final delay, caused by the seaman's strike that was on at the time. However, Roy and I, who had both quit our jobs by then, put the extra two weeks' wait to good use, visiting all but two of the forty-nine pubs in Stratford-on-Avon, where I had been living and working in the last few months leading up to our planned departure.

After one last, big party, which went on until about four o'clock in the morning, we eventually said our final farewells to family and friends on June 17th, 1966 and, each clutching a battered suitcase into which we had packed all our worldly belongings, we boarded the train at Birmingham New Street, bound for Southampton, via London.

My aunt Maud, who lived in London, came to wave us off from the platform at Waterloo. As the train drew out, she wished me 'Bon voyage' and 'Au revoir', adding: "See you again soon." But she got that wrong! It was to be more than fifteen years before we would set eyes on each other again.

Arriving in Southampton, Roy and I were immediately dumbstruck by the sight of all the huge passenger liners and cargo ships down at the quayside. Up until then, the biggest boats we had ever seen were the pleasure cruisers that took tourists up and down the river at Stratford-on-Avon! Having located the M.V. Fairsea, one of the three Sitmar Line cruise ships that regularly carried the £10 Poms to Australia, we were herded into a large shed with our fellow passengers to have our paperwork checked before eventually filing up the gangplank into the vessel that was to be our home for the next five weeks.

Later that afternoon, we were still trying to get settled in down below when the whole ship starting vibrating rather alarmingly and we rushed up on deck to find that we were finally casting off. There were streamers everywhere and with friends and relatives of the 1,700 passengers aboard continuing to wave from the quayside until ship was out of sight, a lot of those hanging over the rail were wiping away a few tears as they shouted their last goodbyes. But not Roy and I. Apart from the fact that nobody from home had come to see us off, we were too excited about what lay ahead to be getting emotional about what we were leaving behind. Looking back for the last time as we passed the Isle of Wight and the coast of England gradually faded into the distance, I thought to myself that there were very few things about my life up until that point that I would miss.

* * * * *

I was born in Lichfield, Staffordshire just after the war ended in 1945. At the time, my father, Dennis Byrne, was working as a shepherd for farmer Denys Stubbs in Swinfen, just outside Lichfield, where we lived in a tied cottage. Of my mother, Frances, I really have no childhood memories whatsoever. I grew up believing that she had been killed during the war. That was what my father had always told me, and for many years I had no reason to doubt him. It wasn't until I was old enough to understand that I had actually been born after the war that it began to dawn on me that his version of events couldn't possibly be true. Even then, I was never told what had really happened – neither by him, nor by my stepmother, Doris. Nicknamed 'Wowey' ever since childhood, because of the way she shouted 'Whoa! Whoa!' to the horses when she was riding on a horse-drawn farm cart, Doris had arrived on the scene when I was six. Up until then I had been looked after at various times by my grandmother and a couple of housekeepers.

I was nearly forty years old before I made the shock discovery that Frances was still very much alive. Far from being killed by a stray German bomb, it turned out that she had actually walked out on the old man when I was three years old. At the same time, I learned, to my further amazement, that I also had two brothers, David and Bob. Frances had taken them with her when she walked out, leaving just me behind for some reason. She had later remarried and had five more children, so I had two half-brothers and three half-sisters as well!

This was all revealed out of the blue one Sunday in 1984 when I got a telephone call from a stranger who announced: "You don't know me, but I'm your brother, Bob!" Until that moment I had not had the slightest hint of his or David's existence, although what he then proceeded to tell me immediately re-awakened in my mind a hazy, almost sub-conscious recollection from my earliest childhood of having stood watching as a woman walked away down our garden path, pushing a pram, with a toddler at her side. Could that have been my first and last memory of my mother and my brothers before they disappeared out of my life?

It may seem extraordinary that it took so long for all this to come out, but you have to understand that my father was not the kind of man you could ever question about things like that and he had obviously sworn the rest of the family to secrecy.

To be quite frank, Dennis Byrne was a pretty nasty piece of work – a brutal, sadistic bully who ruled the household with a rod of iron, whose word was law and who rarely, if ever, showed any affection.

Shortly after he got together with Wowey, he moved us all to Ditchford, a couple of miles outside Shipston, where he had got himself a job managing a 450-acre farm. And from the time I was about eight years old, he had me working with him just about every single hour of the day when I wasn't actually in school. I would have to be up at six every morning, helping to milk the cows and feed the chickens, the pigs and the calves before having breakfast and going off to school. Then, when school finished for the day, I would have to race home as quickly as possible, change into my dungarees and get on with collecting the eggs, mucking out the cow sheds and doing the feeding rounds again. At weekends I worked almost full time. And for all that I got 6d-a-week, rising to 1/- when I was a bit older.

The old man and I would often be working together, side by side, but he never had much to say and would often go for weeks on end without speaking at all. We both knew exactly what jobs had to be done and we got on with them in silence. If I did happen to ask him something, he would answer with a grunt. At the same time he regularly belted me and kicked me around, even for the smallest misdemeanour.

He used to wear a pair of big hob-nailed miner's boots and I can recall more than one occasion when he lost his temper and repeatedly kicked me up the backside so hard that I ended up literally crawling back into the house on all fours. He also had a special way of boxing my ears, cupping his hand to produce a sort of extra thunderclap effect when he whacked me. For some years now I have had to wear a hearing aid and the specialists have told me that those repeated slaps around the head were probably to blame for causing permanent damage to my eardrums.

Wowey used to do her best to protect me and if it hadn't been for her I think I might have gone completely round the bend. As it was, I was so frightened of the old man that I often used to wet my bed.

Also, when I was eight or nine years old, I had to spend five weeks in hospital with mysterious stomach pains. They never did find out exactly what the problem was, but I sometimes wonder if it might have been the beginnings of an ulcer problem that was to plague me later in life, brought on initially by the stress and worry of having to live with such a difficult and domineering father. If Childline had been going in those days, I'd have rung them up and I think they would have taken me away from him – the abuse was that bad.

When I was twelve, Wowey gave birth to a daughter, my half-sister, Bridget. As Bridget grew up, she was also treated pretty badly. At one point she was given a Jack Russell puppy as a pet and one day, when she did something that upset the old man, he grabbed hold of a pitchfork, hooked it under the dog's collar, lifted it up and held it over the fire, saying: "That's where your dog's going to go if you don't behave!" That's the sort of man he was.

Wowey always used to say that it was the cycle of the moon that seemed to affect him. What attracted her to him I'll never know – and many years later she did eventually walk out on him, just as my mother had done. The strange thing was that despite his mean, moody and generally unpleasant manner, he was actually a bit of a ladies' man. He was quite good-looking in a rugged sort of way and whenever he went out, which wasn't that often, he would always be very smartly dressed in a sports jacket, slacks and flat cap that he would get from Esquire, a posh gents' outfitters in Stratford-on-Avon at the time.

By the time he got the farm manager's job at Ditchford, after a brief spell working on another farm in Nuneaton, he was doing quite well for himself. The Ditchford farm was owned by a Mr Morley, a wealthy industrialist from up North who had bought it as an investment and who used to come down and stay there with his family every third weekend or so. He retained half of the big five-bedroom farmhouse for his own use and we lived in the other half. As farm manager and bailiff, the old man was totally responsible for running the place himself and it has to be said that he did a very good job, turning it from a run-down, loss-making concern into a profitable mixed farm, with an AA Attested herd of dairy shorthorns, beef cattle, pigs, sheep, chickens and also turkeys at Christmas.

I grew up fast down on the farm, continuing to work long hours before and after school. By the age of ten, I could pluck a turkey, dress it and have it ready for the oven in less than ten minutes. I started driving tractors at twelve, by which time I was also competent at most country crafts, including hedge laying, hedge brushing and ditching.

From time to time the old man would go to the sales in Ireland to buy beef cattle and to Lerwick and Penrith to buy sheep and I would sometimes be taken along. The animals he bought would be transported down to Moreton-in-Marsh by rail and we would then run them the four or five miles from the station yard straight down the Fosse Way to Ditchford. Imagine trying to do that with today's traffic! There would be five or six of us altogether, blocking off every gateway and side road along the way so as to stop the animals from straying. It would take half-a-day and by the time we got to Ditchford we would have covered a distance of more like ten miles than five, what with all the running backwards and forwards we had to do.

It was exhausting work for the most part, although it did have its funny moments. Working for us in those days was an old shepherd, Ted Wharton, who had a sheep dog called Danny. Ted had lost all his teeth, so he couldn't whistle properly and had to control Danny with a referee's whistle instead. But it kept falling out of his mouth, so Danny didn't know what he was meant to be doing half the time. And whenever a low-flying aircraft came over from the local USAF base, he would chase off after it, barking wildly. There would be Ted, stumbling along the road behind him, frantically blowing his whistle and yelling: "Come back 'ere, Danny, you bugger!"

Such moments of comic relief were fairly few and far between. For the most part, my life outside school hours was just one long, hard grind, seven days a week – week in, week out. We never had any proper holidays. The only time the old man ever took us away was once when he drove us up to Scotland in a Dormobile for a few days – and that was only because he wanted to go and watch some sheep dog trials up there. I had very little spare time to myself and my social life was largely confined to the Young Farmers' Club meetings that took place on a Wednesday evening at the White Horse in Shipston (now The Falcon). I used to ride there on my pushbike and always had to be home by ten o'clock sharp, pedalling like mad to beat the deadline. That curfew continued to be strictly enforced until I left home at seventeen, by which time I was working full-time for the old man.

Although the farm was like a prison in some ways, it also provided my one real escape from the drudgery of the daily routine, with 450 acres to roam around in. From the age of twelve, I had a .410 shotgun with which I would go out shooting for rabbits, pigeons, hares and even the occasional pheasant. The pheasants I mostly poached at night from the farm next door, where there was a four-acre wood in which they used to roost. I would first pop over surreptitiously during the day to clear pathways through the wood, so that I could then creep around after dark without making any noise in the undergrowth, sneaking up on the roosting pheasants and pigeons and picking them off with ease. The best time to go out was on a clear, moonlit night, because the birds would then be silhouetted up in the branches, while down below it would still be so dark that they couldn't see you. Foggy nights were also good, because any sound would be muffled and even if the birds heard a bang, they wouldn't fly very far.

I never got caught. I knew that wood and the rest of my little patch like the back of my hand. Apart from that, the farmer lived about a mile up the road and was very unlikely to be nosing around at that time of night. Also, the old man happened to be on very good terms with our two local bobbies, each of whom would always get a free turkey for Christmas in return for keeping a special eye out on their patrols for any suspicious characters who might be thinking of stealing some of our birds. So, one way and another I felt pretty safe.

The old man knew very well what I was up to, but, for once, he didn't seem to mind me having a bit of fun. As far as I was concerned, it was a nice little sideline that kept me in cartridges and provided a welcome bit of extra spending money. I could get 1/3d for pigeons, 1/6d for rabbits and 2/6d for hares, while pheasants were worth 30/- a brace. I used to sell them to a local shopkeeper in Shipston, never dreaming that one day in the future I myself would own that very same shop.

I left school at sixteen and went to work full-time on the farm – for

£2-a-week! I really wanted to be a carpenter or a cabinet-maker. Woodwork had been my best subject at school and I had also done a course of private study with a firm in Shipston called Williams & Woollett, who, among other things, specialised in producing hand-made elm coffins! It was there that I learned how to achieve that special curved shape of a coffin by making lots of little saw cuts in the boards and then steaming them. I could still do it today. I would have liked to carry on developing my skills in that area, but my father wouldn't hear of it. As far as he was concerned, I was going to be working for him down on the farm and that was the end of it.

At least I had gained a little more freedom by this time, having bought myself a Lambretta motor scooter. This enabled me to get out and about a bit more to see friends, although the 10.00pm curfew was still enforced. Among my friends was a girl called Barbara Walker, whom I had first met at school when I was about fourteen. She lived just this side of Long Compton where her father, Alf Walker, was the local vet. As it happened, her uncle, John Walker, was also a vet, based in Burmington, and John's son, Alan, is now the vet in Hook Norton. Barbara was dark-haired and really cheeky, with a lot to say for herself. She was also a brilliant horse rider, always winning rosettes at local gymkhanas.

As far as I was concerned, it was love at first sight – although in those days, of course, it was all very innocent. There was certainly never any serious kissing and cuddling and we didn't really even go out together that much – my duties at the farm and the curfew imposed by my old man didn't leave much opportunity for that sort of thing. She and her friend Jane Hassell, whose parents owned the Fox and Hounds at Wolford, would sometimes ride over to Ditchford on their ponies. Our first real 'date' was when she and I and Jane and a chap called Pete Steele went to Stratford-on-Avon on the bus to see 'Summer Holiday'. Later, I remember going over to Long Compton on my scooter to pick her up and take her back to my place for tea.

By that time, my father had given up the job as farm manager at Ditchford to take on a place of his own, a council-owned smallhold-ing at Harbury, some distance away, towards Leamington Spa. The round trip to Long Compton was about forty miles, so my relationship with Barbara sort of fizzled out after that, only to be re-ignited in the most extraordinary circumstances more than twenty years later.

I continued to labour for my father for a year after he moved to Harbury and then it was decided that I should go to agricultural college at Moreton Morrell. I didn't want to go – I still fancied being a cabinet-maker – but the old man insisted. The only plus, as far as I was concerned, was that it meant living in at the college and therefore allowed me to get away from home.

At Moreton Morrell you had a choice of two ten-month courses – one that concentrated on livestock and another that focused more on machinery. I chose machinery, partly so that I could get out of milking! I reckoned there wasn't much they could teach me about that side of farming after all the years of hard practical experience I'd had, slaving for my father. In fact, I didn't get out of it altogether because every other weekend you would be on stock duty at the college farm, looking after the animals. And on my weekends off, when I had no option but to go home, I found myself back in the old routine.

It was just as I completed the course in the summer of 1964 and gained my National Certificate that I had a terminal falling out with the old man. That year happened to the first time that The Royal Agricultural Show was held at Stoneleigh, just outside Leamington Spa, and the sponsors, who included *Express Newspapers*, Massey Ferguson, Ford and International Harvester, decided that one of the highlights of the show would be a daily display in the main ring by the so-called Dancing Diggers.

This basically involved eight JCBs doing mechanical dance routines. For a skilled driver, that's not quite as difficult as it might sound. For instance, you could do The Twist simply by raising the machine on its jacks, lowering the bucket and then swivelling the body of the digger from side to side.

Having driven that sort of machinery since I was twelve years old, I had quite an aptitude for it, so I was one of the eight Moreton Morrell students selected to take part in the display, which was to be staged every day during the two weeks that the Show was on.

We spent three weeks beforehand rehearsing and perfecting the various routines, including one in which we were teamed with eight dancers from the Royal School of Ballet. They would do a movement and we would then mimic it in the diggers – and anything they could do, we could do better! It was great fun. We each had our name displayed on the buckets at the back and front of our JCBs and as well as getting all our meals free, we were contracted for two weeks at £10-a-week, which was quite a lot of money at that time. We were also to have the honour of performing in front of the Queen and Prince Philip when they visited the Show.

As the big day approached, we were all getting very excited. But then, at the very last moment, the old man sent Wowey over with the message that he was haymaking at Harbury and needed me at home to help him out. I got on my scooter and drove straight over to explain that there was no way I could let down the rest of the Dancing Diggers team at that late stage and that, anyway, I was under contract for the two weeks. He wouldn't listen and an argument then ensued that ended with him warning me bluntly: "It's either the Royal Show or your job here on the farm – you'd better choose which it's going to be. If you decide to go ahead with the Royal Show, then that's it – you needn't think you can come crawling back here."

"In that case, I'm off," I shouted back angrily. "You can stick your lousy farm job."

I stormed out and that was the last I was to see of my father, or Wowey, for the next sixteen years. As soon as the Royal Show was over, I sold my scooter, bought a Thames van, loaded my few belongings into the back and off I went. I was just nineteen.

I first went to stay with Bob Pick, a friend who was in the same year as me at Moreton Morrell and whose parents had a farm in Warmington, five miles outside Banbury. The Picks kindly offered me temporary bed and board in return for helping out around the farm until I could find myself something more permanent.

After about a week, I managed to fix myself up with a job at Forsyth Farming, a contract farming business that had just started up in Butler's Marston, near Kineton. The work was very hard and involved everything from ploughing, combining and haymaking to hedging and ditching at various farms around the area. My wages were £7-8-0d-a-week, of which £4 went to pay for my board and lodging with Dave

Forsyth, a nephew of old man Forsyth, the gaffer, whose two sons had started the contracting business. It was better than the £2-a-week I had been getting at Harbury, but not much. I was still working seven-days-a-week for very little, but at least I didn't have to put up with my father's bullying manner.

I stayed with Forsyth for the next two years and it was during this period that Roy Pool and I, who had first met up at Moreton Morrell, used to get together on a Friday night at The Horseshoe or The George in Shipston and eventually fell to planning our escape to a brighter and more exciting future. Roy was slaving away on a farm at Darlingscott, where the only consolation was that his boss, Bert Morris, had two very nice daughters! But even that didn't make up for the drudgery of the work and he was as keen as I was to get away.

After we had made our final decision to go off Down Under, and while I was waiting to come of age so that I could sign the necessary papers, I left Forsyth and spent six months with Peak Engineering at Stratford-on-Avon, where I was paid the then princely sum of £30 for just four nights a week. This enabled me to save up quite a bit towards the forthcoming trip – although quite a bit of it disappeared during the extended two-week pub crawl that preceded our delayed departure.

And so it was that I found myself, just days after my 21st birthday, gazing over the rail of the Fairsea without the slightest hint of regret as the coast of England – and, with it, my entire past life – vanished over the horizon.

CHAPTER 2

£10 Pom

The first of many surprises aboard the Fairsea had come when we were shown to our cabin by one of the white-uniformed Italian stewards who had been waiting for us as we came aboard. Any vague illusions we might have been harbouring about a luxury cruise were quickly shattered as the door swung open to reveal a pokey little prison cell of a room. Measuring no more than twelve foot by fourteen, it had six bunk beds ranged around the walls, a single porthole about twelve inches across and three very small wardrobes, to be shared by all six occupants.

As Roy and I were the first in, we had the pick of the bunks and chose the lower ones, figuring that we would not have quite so far to fall if we were thrown out in bad weather. Next to arrive were Jim and John, from Liverpool. Like just about every other young man from that part of the world in the days when Beatlemania was still at its peak, they had been members of a rock band and their suitcases were crammed full of trendy gear, which only added to the problem of wardrobe space. They were typical Scousers, a couple of scallywags with heavy Liverpool accents and a great sense of humour.

Then there was Mel, from London. He was very quiet and had bright ginger hair, which was quite useful because it helped to distinguish him from the sixth occupant, who was also called Mel, but who was very different to look at, being very tall, with dark hair. He soon turned out to be a right comedian and was quite happy to have one of the top bunks, his long legs enabling him to get in and out quite easily without stepping on the person below.

With all the introductions made and the cabin arrangements

sorted out, it was time to start exploring the rest of the ship, our main priorities being to find out where the bars were and to eye up the 'talent' among our fellow passengers.

We were delighted to find that there were no less than three bars and even more pleasantly surprised to discover that, being duty free, a can of beer cost only a shilling while cigarettes were just 1/3d for twenty. We then located the dining room, where we were informed that there would be two sittings for dinner – at 6.30pm and eight o'clock. Although we were starving, we opted to wait for the second sitting on the grounds that the earlier one would probably be full of kids and families. Apart from that, we were worried that it might also interfere with our late afternoon sunbathing up on deck.

As for the 'birds', we had already spotted quite a few highly fanciable young ladies coming aboard, so Roy and I decided to dress up that first night in order to impress. With jeans and T-shirts swapped for our best drainpipe trousers, fashionable winkle-picker shoes and crisp white Marks & Sparks shirts, unbuttoned to reveal more than a hint of suntan and hairy chest, we reckoned we must look the business – a right couple of likely lads!

We went along to the dining room early, keen to secure a good table and anticipating long queues and a bit of a crush given that roughly half of the 1,700 passengers aboard would presumably be descending on the restaurant for each sitting. We needn't have worried. We arrived to find the place nearly deserted – and it didn't take too long to figure out why. The sea was already getting a bit choppy by this time and, with no stabilisers, the Fairsea was starting to roll quite a bit with the swell. As we walked into the empty dining room, the first thing we saw were some large bowls of cold consommé soup sitting on a side table, swilling gently from side to side as the ship moved. For anyone feeling in the least bit queasy this must have been the final straw. Luckily, both Roy and I turned out to be good sailors right from the start and suffered no ill effects at all. We tucked into a very good four-course meal, as we did every evening from then on.

Dinner over, we returned to the bar up on the sun deck. By this time, however, the weather was getting really rough as we headed into the Bay of Biscay, so we walked around to the less windy side of the ship and went in search of an inside bar. It was now that we found out where all the absent diners were – hanging over the lea side rail and not feeling at all well! Half the Italian crew seemed to be out there with them, mopping up the deck!

Things got even worse that night and our cabin being right at the front end of the boat, we took the brunt of the weather, lurching up and down quite violently. It didn't bother me too much – I actually found that it helped to rock me to sleep! In fact, 'Ginger' Mel was the only one of us who really suffered badly.

The next day was just as uncomfortable as we ploughed on across the Bay of Biscay, with an awful lot of people looking very green about the gills and making regular dashes for the rail. Poor devils! Once again, the dining room was almost completely empty. It wasn't until the third or fourth day, as we rounded Cape St Vincent and passed through the Straits of Gibraltar into the Mediterranean, that things eventually settled down and most people began to get their sea legs.

With meal times now better attended, we were able to start making friends with our fellow passengers and little groups began to form. We were seated eight to a table, each with its own waiter, and regular tables were soon established. It wasn't long before Roy and I hooked up with Vera and Dot, two girls from Manchester. Roughly the same age as us, they, too, had decided that they needed to get out of the rut in which they had found themselves back at home and, keen to see a bit of the world, were planning to go out to Oz for maybe just a couple of years.

I found myself immediately attracted to Vera, a gorgeous brunette with a stunning figure. And once we got chatting, it soon became clear that we actually had quite a lot in common. Like me, she had not got on well with a domineering father, a pipe major in the Irish Guards who, by all accounts, could be a bit of a bully. Also like me, she had felt trapped in a job with no real prospects, working on the switchboard at Manchester United. That was not anywhere near as glamorous or exciting as it might possibly sound to some. She and Dot were best friends who had been at school together. And, just as Roy and I had done, they had both made up their minds to find a new life for themselves.

From the moment Vera and I first got together that was it as far as I was concerned. I didn't have eyes for anyone else on board for the rest of the voyage. Roy and the others, however, decided to play the field – and there was certainly plenty of opportunity for that. There was so much shipboard romance that the Fairsea should probably have been re-named 'The Love Boat'. One of the stranger aspects of life aboard was the fact that there were no mixed-sex cabins, so that couples, even husbands and wives, were split up. Almost inevitably, this led to all sorts of shenanigans. By the time we'd been at sea for two or three weeks, it seemed as if everybody was at it! If you took a turn around the deck after dark you were liable to come across couples making love wherever they could find a bit of cover – even in the lifeboats. And they weren't always with the person they should have been with!

Things started warming up – in every sense – as soon as we got into the Mediterranean. The days were filled with all kinds of organised deck games, as well as lots of sunbathing and swimming. And every night there were parties, dances and discos, all of this fuelled by the ready availability of cheap duty free booze.

The swimming pool was in the shaft that formed the entrance to the hold. This was sealed and filled with seawater, creating a pool that measured about thirty foot square and fifteen foot deep. A safety net was put over it at night and this was used as a trampoline during the informal parties that took place at the end of every evening after the regular dance, disco or cabaret performance had finished. There was quite a big group of us now who would gather and sit up on deck until the early hours of the morning, chatting, singing and indulging in such sophisticated pursuits as seeing who could throw an empty beer car furthest over the side of the ship. If you wanted to cheat, you could half fill the can with water from the swimming pool when nobody was watching. It would often be dawn before these get-togethers broke up and as a result our lot only made it to breakfast about three times in the entire five weeks we were at sea.

The sunbathing was going so well that we soon started to look more like Aborigines than Poms. Only 'Big' Mel – as distinct from

'Ginger' Mel – overdid it. He fell asleep on deck one afternoon and lay there for four hours in the full sun. When he eventually came down to the cabin he looked like a lobster and we had to lay him out on a lower bunk and bathe him with cold tea. Two days later we were peeling the skin off his back like sheets of tissue paper.

It was shortly after this that we arrived at our first port of call – Port Said. By this time, we were all looking forward to getting back on dry land again. As soon as we tied up, the ship was surrounded by Arab traders in small boats, all trying to sell us their wares. Also swimming about in the water below us were dozens of children, waving to us and encouraging us to throw coins overboard so that they could dive and retrieve them. They were very good at this and managed to make themselves quite a bit of pocket money.

The purser on board the Fairsea had organised a special sightseeing trip from Port Said to Cairo, with those who took part re-joining the ship at Suez. The cost of this three-day excursion, which included two nights in a hotel in Cairo, was just £8-a-head. And although it meant we would miss the experience of going through the Suez canal, we reckoned it was worth it, so Vera and I and just about everybody else in our group of friends jumped at the chance.

Leaving the Fairsea, we all filed onto coaches and set off through the desert towards Cairo. Here, the temperature was up near the 100°F mark. I don't think any of us had ever been abroad before, so it was all very new to us and along the way we gazed in fascination as we passed numerous camels laden with all sorts of produce, including mostly watermelons, dates, bananas and the reeds used to thatch the mud huts in which a lot of the people lived. At one point, right out in the middle of nowhere, we came across an encampment of tents. Our guide explained that this was an army unit, out on a training exercise, and I remember wondering how they could possibly survive in that intense heat, without any shade to provide relief.

By the time we arrived in Cairo we were hot, sweaty and dusty and dying for a cool shower. We had been booked into the Hotel Carlton, a very impressive high rise building, and after freshening up we all went out for a meal in a local Egyptian restaurant. The waiters there were dressed in long white robes, with fezes on their heads, and I don't know what was worse – their B.O problem or the steak they gave us to eat. I'm sure it must have been camel!

After dinner, we decided to have a look around. We had been warned not, on any account, to go out on the streets of Cairo at night, but we reckoned there would be safety in numbers and went for a short walk before returning to the roof garden bar of the hotel for a few cold beers in what was still stifling heat, even after dark. It was only when we got up there that we realised just how tall the hotel building was. You could see all over Cairo, the lights seeming to stretch forever into the distance. The setting was very romantic and I think it was probably at that moment that my relationship with Vera was sealed.

The temperature remained high throughout the night, the ceiling fan simply blowing hot air everywhere. This made it difficult to sleep and we were up early the next morning for breakfast. After the experience of the night before, we decided it would be safer and more sensible to opt for the 'continental' breakfast.

Next on our itinerary was a visit to Giza to see the Pyramids and the Sphinx. We all piled into the coach and even though it was still very early, the sun was already beating down and getting hotter by the minute. By the time we arrived at Giza, we were roasting. There were dozens of camels standing around with their owners and we were immediately surrounded by beggars, holding out their hands and endlessly repeating: "Sugar for the camel, sugar for the camel!" Our guide quickly taught us a very useful word for such situations. Pronounced phonetically 'Emshee', it was obviously the equivalent of **** off! Partly to escape the attentions of the persistent beggars, some of us decided to take a camel ride for the few hundred yards to the Pyramids. It only cost the equivalent of two shillings and saved walking on the burning hot sand.

The Pyramids were much bigger than I had imagined they would be and were very impressive in their construction. We clambered up a few steps of the main one and were then guided into a long passageway that led to a chamber right in the middle. This was where the ancient pharaohs were buried. There was a rather funny smell about the place – but at least it was a bit cooler in there.

After a long lecture on the history of the Pyramids we went back down the passageway to the glare and heat of the desert. From there we moved on to the Sphinx, the great stone statue that looks a bit like a lion with a woman's head. The best thing about this was that it did afford a bit of shade if you stood in the right spot. But there was nothing you could do about the flies. They were particularly irritating, crawling around your eyes and mouth. And we didn't even have hats with which to swat them away. One way and another, we were all quite relieved when the time came to crawl back on the coach and head back to town.

However, our sightseeing for the day was still not over. Our guide had also organised a trip around a large street market on the outskirts of Cairo. This turned out to be a really interesting experience. The market comprised literally hundreds of stalls, selling just about everything you could possibly think of. The goods on offer ranged from fresh fruit and vegetables to carpets and livestock of every description, herbs, spices and perfumed oils.

There were also lots of young boys going around selling bottles of Coca Cola, which were kept cool with dry ice. As with everything else, you could haggle over the price. You never paid the asking price for anything. Meanwhile, the guide was always on hand to make sure you weren't robbed. You had to watch your wallet constantly. The eyes of the street urchins and everybody else in the crowded market were constantly alert, watching your every movement and, we were warned, waiting for the opportunity to relieve you of your valuables.

We spent a fascinating couple of hours in the market, taking in all the wonderfully exotic sights and sounds and enjoying the most truly foreign atmosphere that any of us had experienced up until then. We even risked sampling some of the food that was on offer from the many street stalls, thankfully without any ill effects.

Back at the hotel we revived ourselves with long, cool showers before going down to the lounge bar. The beer wasn't brilliant, but it was safer than the water. The girls were told not even to have ice in their drinks, just in case the water it was made from was dodgy.

We sat around swapping tales about the experiences we'd had during the day and then went in to dinner in the hotel restaurant. It was noticeable that, even there, nobody had 'steak' that night, most people opting for salad and fruit salad. Although we went slightly hungry as a result, we consoled ourselves with the thought that we could make up for it with a good feed when we got back on the ship.

The usual gang were back up in the beer garden after dinner. By this time it included Phil, an engineer from Lancashire who was slightly older than the rest of us and a bit more serious. He had hooked up with Dot.

Just as we had been plagued by flies during the day, at night it was the turn of the mosquitoes to torment us. They could be real pests. Fortunately, we did have mozzie nets over the beds, but, even so, the strain of listening out for the telltale, high-pitched buzz that meant one had got through the net, combined with the oppressive heat, meant that it was very difficult to get much sleep.

Our final day in Cairo was taken up with a visit to the local museum and to a mosque. We went first to the museum, which was housed in a marvellously impressive building. Apart from all the illustrated history and the displays of ancient artefacts, there was a whole section devoted to the tomb of a pharaoh. This featured a breathtaking array of solid gold items that had been found in the Pyramids. We spent nearly four hours looking around, but could quite happily have spent four days there – and even then we would still not have had time to see everything and to learn as much as we would have liked to know about the country's history.

Last on our agenda was the visit to the mosque. Not being religious, Roy and I went along without a great deal of enthusiasm. When we got there, the first thing we had to do was to take off our shoes and leave them at the entrance. How the locals ever found their own shoes again I'll never know, since all their sandals looked exactly the same to me.

Inside the mosque it seemed to be strictly men only, all of them kneeling down with their foreheads pressed to the floor and their backsides in the air, while someone chanted endlessly, sounding as though he had some kind of gut ache. What a strange religion, we thought. Back outside once more, we were shown into a courtyard where all the men were walking up to a wall and kissing it. To one side was another wall with an archway and we were told that this was the wishing arch. You had to walk through it and make a wish and if you put a silver coin in the box, your wish would come true. I put sixpence in the box and made a wish – never imagining for one moment that it would be granted. But it was. That sixpence turned out to be the best tanner I'd ever spent, as will be revealed later!

Leaving the mosque, we boarded the coaches and headed for Suez. More desert, more heat – we didn't even stop for refreshment. Not that there was anywhere to stop along the way. When we eventually got to Suez, a journey of sixty or seventy miles, it was a relief to get back on the ship. We went straight to the dining room for a meal and then up to the sun deck for a decent beer or three! They weren't supposed to serve any booze until we left port, but by this time we had established a very good relationship with one of the barmen and he was happy to bend the rules. It was late afternoon by this time and still very hot, so we sat up on the sun deck until it got dark, watching all the activity as we slipped out of Suez and down the Gulf of Suez. This seemed for a while like a very wide river, with nothing but sand dunes on either side. As night fell, we could occasionally glimpse the twinkling lights of small towns or villages on the shores, but, even so, it seemed like a very desolate place.

We soon slipped back into the usual routine of sunbathing, swimming and organised deck games during the day, followed by dinner at eight, dancing to the ship's resident band or a disco and then up onto the sun deck, armed with few packs of beers, for a chat and a sing-song under the stars, these sessions usually going on until the very early hours.

By now everybody in the gang seemed to have paired off. Apart from Vera and I, there were Phil and Dot, Liz and Norman – and even Roy's roving eye seemed to have settled at last on Patricia. The Scousers, Jim and John, and the two Mels had also found girlfriends. Also in our group were a couple of Aussies, who were on their way home after an extended stay in England and on the Continent. They kept us amused by teaching us a few Aussie slang words and phrases, many of which remain unprintable. Girls, we learned, were always 'Sheilas', 'Durex' was cellotape (one could imagine a few embarrassing misunderstandings there!) and a 'technicolour yawn' was what you were likely to experience when the motion of the boat sent you dashing for the side. As for the many curses they taught us, the one that had us all in fits was: "I hope your chooks turn to emus and kick your ******* dunny down!" This roughly translates as: "I hope your chickens turn into emus (fearsomely aggressive birds with a kick like a mule) and destroy your outside toilet!" As I was to appreciate once I got out into the bush, the loss of one's outside loo facility was the sort of major domestic catastrophe that you would only wish on your worst enemy.

As we continued south into the Red Sea it got warmer and warmer. Even at night, it didn't cool down until about four in the morning. Our days got lazier and lazier. It was too hot for deck games and you had to be very careful about how much time you spent in the full sun. Extra entertainment was provided by the dolphins that attached themselves to the ship, swimming alongside and playing in the bow wave, and by the flying fish that could occasionally be seen skimming the waves. We had all heard or read about them, but until we saw them for the first time we couldn't believe that they could actually stay airborne for forty or fifty yards at a time. Occasionally, we were told, they flew so high that they would end up on the lower decks of ships.

The temperature continued to rise steadily until we reached Aden. We berthed there at five o'clock one morning and by 9.00am it was already over 120°. What a place that was! Surrounded by bare granite rocks that seemed to both absorb and reflect the sun's rays, it was like a cauldron of sizzling heat.

This was during the time of the Aden Emergency, the result of political unrest caused by insurgents in the period following the colony's incorporation into the Federation of Arab Emirates of the South in 1963 and during the run-up to independence in 1968. British Army units were patrolling the streets and although we were allowed ashore, all of us stayed well within the safe area around the port itself. All of us except Roy, that is! He was determined to visit the area known as The Crater, the main trouble spot. This was considered especially dangerous, but Roy eventually found a taxi driver who was prepared to take him on a guided tour. I told him there was no way I was going with him – and was quite relieved when he returned safely about two hours later.

The risk he had taken was underlined moments later when there was a loud explosion as a shop front was blown out by insurgents. At that point, everybody decided that it was time to get back on board the Fairsea. We were only too happy to leave that God-forsaken place behind and I think we all heaved a sigh of relief when the ship eventually cast off and headed out into the Indian Ocean.

We now had another two-and-a-half weeks to go before our next stop. This would be at Fremantle, our first landfall in Australia. By now, we had started devising our own entertainments on board. We had got together with the purser and the resident band and arranged to have different theme nights for the dances, complete with makeshift fancy dress. First, we decided to have a Roman night. We all dressed up in bed sheets and sandals and, for some reason, seemed to spend a lot of time singing 'When The Saints Go Marching In'. That went down very well, although Roy, for one, was certainly no saint!

As usual, we had adjourned to the top deck when the dance ended and after a while I noticed that Roy was missing. Thinking that he might be unwell, I thought I had better go off to look for him and went first to check our cabin. Switching on the light and looking across to his bunk, I was confronted by the sight of a bare backside sticking out between the curtains that could be drawn across the front to provide a bit of privacy. I gave it a playful slap only to realise, an instant too late, that it didn't belong to Roy!

After being treated to a barrage of bad language from his lady friend, I departed quickly and re-joined the others on the top deck. We all had a good laugh about it later and even his girlfriend eventually saw the funny side of it. I, myself, was never caught in quite such a compromising situation although Vera and I did get a telling off from the captain after he spotted us having a kiss and cuddle up on deck late one night. I thought that was a bit strong given that we all knew that he himself was having a fling with one of the passengers. As I mentioned earlier, the ship was like a floating brothel by this stage, with almost everybody enjoying a bit of romance.

The next big party was organised as part of the traditional cere-mony of 'crossing the line', the moment when we passed over the Equator and into the southern hemisphere. For first timers the cere-mony involved being covered with shaving foam and shaved by Neptune before then being thrown into the swimming pool. Need-less to say, the shaving foam tended to end up in all sorts of interest-ing places!

Later that evening there was a special 'Crossing The Line Dinner'.

The chef had excelled himself, serving up about seven courses alto-gether. Afterwards there was a dance. Jim and John, our guitar-playing Liverpudlian cabin-mates, soon hi-jacked the band so that only the original drummer was left, with others among our gang taking turns to play the tambourine. From then on it rapidly developed into a riotous party, one of the high points of the whole voyage.

A few days after this, Roy rousted me out of bed early one morning, shouting: "Get up quick! There's a clay pigeon shooting competition on the top deck!"

Bleary-eyed, I staggered out into the bright sunshine. Sure enough, they had a trap set up on the railings at the rear of the ship. The sea was a bit choppy, so you had to pick your moment to shout: "Pull!" But having done a fair bit of shooting back on the farm, both Roy and I thought we'd stand a chance of winning. We were allowed five shots each and duly got rid of the opposition, so that it ended up as a shoot-out between the two of us, with me eventually winning by one shot. There was a presentation at the usual dinner and dance that evening, but all I got as first prize was a cheap wallet, which was hardly worth it after the money I'd had to spend on cartridges.

Out in the middle of the Indian Ocean, the sea became very rough again over the next few days as we got caught up in a tropical cyclone, the ship crashing head-on through forty-foot waves. At night, you had to hang on tight to avoid getting thrown out of your bunk and during the day even walking around was quite difficult as the vessel lurched and rolled. I was worried that one leg would end up shorter than the other! Fortunately, most of us had got our sea legs by this time, but, even so, some people suffered badly with seasickness.

Thankfully, the weather cleared after about three days, the sunshine returned and we were back in cruise mode. Throughout the trip there was a daily competition to guess how many miles we had travelled in the previous twenty-four hours, but I never got close to winning. We all reckoned that the storm must have slowed us up a bit. There was then another unexpected problem when one of the ship's two engines packed up, reducing us to half-speed. After a day or so, the other engine also stopped. Nobody seemed to panic, but with no ventilation in the cabins it became very hot and stuffy down below and we took to sleeping up on deck. Our main concern was to make sure that the beer supplies stayed cold!

It took about two days for the ship's engineers to fix the problem and then we were off again on what was to be the last lap of our long voyage. We reckoned it was just as well that we were nearing journey's end as we were fast running out of fresh ideas for the themed dances that we had been continuing to run on a nightly basis!

We hadn't seen land for more than a fortnight and there was great excitement as we got closer and closer to our destination. Everybody was scanning the horizon, eagerly anticipating the first glimpse of Oz. At last the cry went up and we all strained our eyes, trying to make out the faint smudge on the skyline that then gradually changed from grey to blue to black before coming into sharper focus as we neared Fremantle, our first port of call on the coast of Western Australia.

For almost exactly five weeks we had been suspended in a state of very enjoyable limbo as we sailed into the unknown. Many of us had left our homeland and set out with no clear idea of exactly what we would find when we finally stepped ashore at the other end, although our imaginations had been working overtime. Would it be the promised land of milk and honey, of endless sunshine, white sand beaches and a wonderfully laid-back outdoor lifestyle? Or would it be like some extended frontier town from the Old American West, with kangaroos hopping along down dusty high streets? And grizzled Aussie bastards, with corks dangling from the brims of sweat-stained bush hats, lying in wait in every saloon bar, desperate for any excuse to give the 'whingeing Poms' a bloody good hiding? The truth was about to be revealed.

CHAPTER 3

Down Under

It was midwinter in Fremantle when we arrived there at the end of July, although you would never have guessed it. The weather was beautiful, the average winter temperature in Western Australia being a very pleasant 18°C (just under 70°F), and many of the wild flowers for which the state is famed were in full bloom.

For some of the passengers aboard the Fairsea this was the final destination and while they were being dropped off to start their new lives, Roy and I and the rest of the gang took the opportunity to grab a taxi at the quayside and head into Perth, just a few miles inland, to have a quick look around before we sailed on. Trish, who had lived there before, became our elected guide as we did a whistle-stop tour of what must be the cleanest city in the world. That, at least, was our over-riding first impression.

For me, the highlight of this brief sightseeing trip was our visit to the botanical gardens. Here, as we admired sweeping views out across the Swan River, Trish was able to identify and point out all the native sub-tropical trees and shrubs, including bougainvillaea, hibiscus, poinsettia and frangipani, the dazzling array of colours adding an exotic touch to the landscape.

We barely had time to take it all in before we were back on the ship, continuing on across the Great Australia Bight to the next stop. With fewer passengers now on board, we were able to move into a cabin nearer the middle of the ship. Apart from being more comfortable, this had the added advantage of being only a few doors away from the girls' cabin. And, being on very friendly terms by this time, we soon re-organised the sleeping arrangements!

After a couple of days, we arrived in Adelaide and, once again, our group popped into the city centre to take a quick look around while the next batch of our fellow passengers were being off-loaded. This time we went by tram. Adelaide gave the impression of being older than Perth, although just as clean and tidy. It was also a bit cooler.

Our next port of call was Melbourne, just a day's sailing away. A lot less clean and much busier, this was not nearly so much to our liking and we were quite relieved to get back aboard the Fairsea for the final, two-day leg to Sydney.

In some ways, we were sad to be nearing the end of our long voyage. We'd had a marvellous time on the ship, had made some good friends and had seen and done many interesting and different things. Our home for well over a month, the Fairsea had been our one remaining link with the past, as it were. Now it was time to step into the unknown and a brand new life. After dinner on our last night aboard, we had a final farewell party 'up top'. It was quite an emotional occasion for all of us.

We managed only a couple of hours sleep before arriving in Sydney Harbour at about five o'clock in the morning. Despite the pre-dawn chill and some fairly thick heads, the inevitable hangover from the night before, we made our way up onto the deck and lined the rail to watch as the ship eased her way under the world-famous Sydney Harbour Bridge. Even in the semi-darkness, its outline was immediately recognisable from the pictures we had all seen. The lights on the bridge were very impressive, as were those of the city itself, twinkling far into the distance beyond. As dawn broke, early morning ferries were already busily criss-crossing the harbour.

As the ship docked, we raced down below to finish packing, but then had to wait until the customs and immigration officials were ready before we could eventually disembark. As we came down the gangplank we were then herded into a large corrugated iron building where we queued up, waiting to go through the various formalities. Somebody told the old joke about the man arriving in Australia for the first time who was rather surprised to be asked if he had a criminal record. "Do you still have to have one to get into this place?" he quipped – and was immediately sent to the back of the queue by a humourless official.

Having successfully passed through the immigration process, it was time for another round of emotional farewells as the gang split up to go their separate ways. Vera and Dot were among those going on up to Brisbane, as were Trish and Gordon. Roy and I, on the other hand, had elected to stay in Sydney.

We had been given no clear idea before we set out from England about exactly what would be happening to us once we arrived in Australia, simply that we would be allocated temporary rented accommodation while we settled in and looked around for jobs. It was only as we passed through immigration that we learned we were being sent to a sort of hostel-cum-boarding-house at Parramatta, a suburb about seventeen miles west of the city centre that turned out to have been one of the first convict settlements in Australia back in the 18th century. A lot of the bridges and various public facilities in the area had little plaques on them, recording that they had been 'Built By Convict Labour'.

Along with three others, we piled into a taxi and headed off there. The hostel turned out to be comprised of a modern, two-storey, brick-built house with a couple of weatherboard chalets round the back. The main house looked quite nice, but we were put into one of the chalets, which weren't quite so good. In fact, they were real doss houses. We were sleeping three to a room and with only one blanket each we soon found that winter nights in Sydney can be uncomfortably chilly. Even worse than the cold were the bed bugs.

The first night was a complete nightmare. Not only were we freezing, we were also bitten half to death. There was only one way to deal with the bugs. You had to jump out of bed in the dark and get a wet bar of soap. You then switched on the light, threw back the bedclothes and dabbed at the bugs with the bar of soap so that they stuck to it. The next morning, we headed straight down to the local shops to get some insect killer.

We got quite a surprise in the first shop that we went into. Behind the counter was a Chinaman, who greeted us in traditional Australian fashion with a friendly: "G'day, mate". Despite his appearance, he sounded more Aussie than the Aussies themselves!

Having armed ourselves with bed bug repellent and other essential supplies such as beer and cigarettes – the favourite Aussie brand was Winfield – it was time to start looking for a job. I had set out from England with about £300, but most of this had been spent on the way over and by the time we got off the ship all I had to my name was enough for about two weeks' rent plus a few Australian dollars.

We went down to the local job centre every day for the first few days, but there was nothing doing there. It turned out there had been a seven-year drought in the country and, as a result, the economy had suffered and jobs were scarce. So much for the promised land of milk and honey! It seemed that the cows had gone dry and the bees had flown off.

Determined, on principle, not to go on the dole, we then started doing the rounds of local businesses and after a brief stint as casual labourers on a land clearance project at a new industrial estate, we eventually landed regular part-time jobs loading trucks for the local newspaper a couple of nights a week. Ten dollars-a-night for a shift that lasted from 9pm to 6am seemed like peanuts, especially as we were paying A$13-a-week for board and lodging. The one advantage was that we got to see the 'Jobs Vacant' section in the paper before anyone else. As a result, Roy soon found himself a job with a construction company while I went to work full-time for a second hand car dealer, steam cleaning and re-spraying cars. This meant walking more than a mile to and from work each day, but I didn't mind that at all. I actually enjoyed walking through the suburbs first thing in the morning, past all the lovely gardens, listening to the extraordinary and rather comical call of the kookaburra. The Australian equivalent of a kingfisher, this bird is known as the 'laughing jackass' on account of its highly unusual cry, which actually sounds uncannily like a human laugh.

Once we had settled in and had a bit of money in our pockets, Roy and I decided it was time to start exploring, to find out more about our new environment and the wildlife. Our first major trip was up to Katoomba in the Blue Mountains, one of the region's main tourist attractions, about eighty miles inland from Sydney. We had no transport of our own at this time so we went up by train.

This was our first taste of the Australian Outback – the bush, as they call it. Once past Penrith, we soon spotted our first kangaroo, which caused great excitement. We also saw emus and a whole lot of quite exotic birdlife, including rose-breasted galah cockatoos and parrots.

Katoomba itself was awe-inspiring, with stunning views from Echo Point and out over the spectacular rock formation known as The Three Sisters. We were told that the scenic walk down the Giant Stairway into the Jamison Valley below was well worth doing and Roy decided that we should give it a try. We set off with great enthusiasm, but what they hadn't told us was that the descent involved a flight of eight hundred stone steps! By the time we had climbed back up to the Tourist Centre at Echo Point we were completely knackered. To make matters worse, all the bars there were closed, it being a Sunday, so we had to make do with coke!

By this time, we were already well into Australia's notorious drinking culture. We had got a taste of what it was like when we first started work in the newspaper plant. The pubs in the area would open at 6am to cater for workers on the surrounding industrial estate coming off the night shift. They would then be joined a little later on by commuters on their way to the railway station to catch a train to the city centre. We would always drop in for a couple of beers when our shift finished at six, our excuse being that this helped you to sleep during the day. But it seemed weird to see these blokes dressed in pinstripe suits and carrying briefcases come in for a drink on their way in to work!

The next stage in our education came when we ventured for the first time into King's Cross, Sydney's answer to London's Soho. In terms of décor, the bars and nightclubs there were far superior to anything around in England at the time – all modern stainless steel and glass. But in most other respects the riotous, free-for-all atmosphere in these places made the rowdiest Saturday night rugby club bar in the UK look by comparison like the cocktail lounge at the Savoy Hotel.

To speed up service, beer was normally dispensed through beer guns. Think petrol pumps! The barmen would line up ice-frosted pint glasses on the bar and literally hose the beer into them, a dozen at a time. On a busy Saturday night the whole place would soon be awash with beer. The stone floor would have a drain running down the middle and at the end of the evening, once everybody had left and gone home, the staff would simply come in with a high-powered hose and sluice it down.

The actual bars were raised high and were also very wide, simply to prevent angry customers from leaning across and hanging one on the barmen if things turned nasty – which they often did in the scramble to get served amid the crush. If you were half sensible, mind you, you wouldn't even want to mess with the barmaids down there, let alone the barmen.

There were always enormous bouncers on the door and a lot of the pubs – or hotels, as they call them out there – wouldn't let you in unless you had a female with you, the idea being that this would help to keep down the fighting. As a result, you'd often have to hang around outside, chatting up unattached girls just to get in. Even so, there would often be the most terrible punch-ups. Despite those comic adverts you see on TV, it's certainly no joke when it comes to the Aussies and their beer. And those Sydney bars, in particular, were a riot. After The Horseshoe in Shipston, it really was like entering a completely different world.

Despite their occasionally abrasive manner, we got on really well with the Aussies, who have a great sense of humour and genuinely don't seem to give a **** about anything. Their generally laid-back manner used to be perfectly reflected in the popular expression 'Leave it to Ron' – later on, that is. And the idea that all Brits are regarded as 'whingeing Poms' is misleading. Sadly, a lot of the people who emigrated out there at that time in the hope of finding a better and easier life were actually the sort of failures who had never done any good at home in the UK and were never going to do any good anywhere else. They had gone out thinking that the streets really would be paved with gold and then, when they found it wasn't quite that easy, they started complaining about all and sundry, always going on about how much better things were back home. That's where that whole whingeing Pom thing came from. Because Roy and I were determined to make a go of it out there, we were very careful not to blather on about England. We just tried to forget it existed. As a result, we never came up against any hostility from the locals.

Back at Parramatta we had got friendly with a truck driver called Bob, who was living in the main boarding house. Bob was a member of the Parramatta Leagues Club, a local sports and social club that was just across the road from the boarding house, and after he had taken us over there a few times we became associate members. Apart from cheap beer and bars on three different floors, the club featured about one hundred-and-forty 'pokie machines', what we call one-armed bandits in this country. Quite a bit of our loose change ended up in those machines.

There would be a cabaret act every Saturday evening and at eleven o'clock on Sunday mornings there was what was known as 'the sick parade'. This was not, as the name might suggest, a get-together of those suffering hangovers from the night before and in need of 'the hair of the dog', but a 'men only' cabaret, featuring some fairly outrageous female impersonators.

This sort of thing was extremely popular in Australia, which rather surprised us because we'd always thought of the Aussies as being an especially butch, macho lot.

Not all our spare time was spent in the clubs and bars. We were also continuing to explore the area and, as country boys, we had a special interest in the local flora and fauna. After our visit to Katoomba, our next outdoor trip was a walk around the fringes of Parramatta Lake. This turned out to be a five-mile nature ramble. We had heard some lurid stories about the many deadly snakes and spiders that are to be found in Australia and kept a wary eye out at first for slithering creepy crawlies, but although the wildlife was abundant, we spotted nothing more fearsome-looking than a large lizard, which we spent some time trying to catch, without success. He was much too quick for us.

By mid-day it was getting quite warm, so I decided to go for a swim. I hadn't brought any trunks or a towel, but thought that I would go in wearing my shorts and then dry off in the sun afterwards. However, I got a shock when I dived in. Although it looked very inviting, the water was bloody freezing! I couldn't wait to get out. Roy thought this was hilarious – until a few minutes later when we were walking along some rocks on the shore and I managed to push him in. He took a dim view of that, but was forced to agree about the temperature of the water.

We had kept in touch with some other members of the gang from the Fairsea who had ended up in the centre of Sydney and, after a week or so, we decided to organise a party. We hopped on the train and headed for the city, where we first went to look up a girl called Maggie Duff, who was living with some friends in Cremorne, a very posh area overlooking Sydney Harbour. It certainly made Parramatta look very second rate and as we headed back there after much partying and the downing of many 'coldies', we began to think that maybe we had drawn the short straw.

This feeling was reinforced when we returned the following weekend and stayed overnight. After another big party on the Saturday night, we headed out across the Sydney Harbour Bridge on Sunday, bound for Bondi Beach. Going across the bridge, it was immediately obvious why the locals called it 'the coathanger'. As for Bondi, it more than lived up to its advance reputation, with miles of golden sand, a beautiful turquoise sea, crashing surf and gorgeous, suntanned bodies in very brief bikinis all over the place.

Back down to earth at the Parramatta boarding house, we had at least moved out of the chalet and into the main building, which was much more comfortable. The food, however, was still pretty awful – cereal and toast for breakfast, peanut butter sandwiches for lunch and stew for supper. The menu was exactly the same every day of the week. In desperation, we would often skip supper and go over to the Leagues Club for a decent steak and chips.

One way and another, Roy and I were beginning to get restless and, after seeing an advert in the local paper, we applied to join the police force up in the Northern Territory. An area as big as France, Italy and Spain put together, this is the wildest and most remote region of Australia. Sparsely populated and with an environment that ranges from the lush, green tropical steam heat of the so-called Top End around the capital, Darwin, to the harsh, arid desert of the Red Centre, it is home to some of the country's most extreme wildlife and also to most of its native Aborigines. It is here that you find several of Australia's best-known landmarks, including Ayers Rock, Kings Canyon and the town of Alice Springs. As a child, Roy had once seen a television documentary about it called Under The Northern Star, presented by the husband-and-wife team Armand and Michaela Dennis, and it made such a deep impression on him that from that moment on it had always been his ambition to go there himself one day.

After sending off our applications, we were both called in for an interview and medical. Two weeks later, we heard that although Roy had been accepted, I had been rejected because I was half-an-inch too short! In the meantime, Vera and Dot had been in touch from Brisbane to say that they had heard through Trish, whose family lived in the area, about a couple of jobs that were going up there on farms, or 'properties' as the Australians call them. Roy had already made up his mind that he was going to give the police force a go and as I couldn't go with him I decided to try my luck in Queensland.

Roy and I said our goodbyes at the railway station in Sydney and went our separate ways, never thinking that it would be more than twenty years before we saw each other again. Nor could we ever have imagined the stories we would have to tell each other when we were eventually re-united in the very same bar back in Shipston-on-Stour where the great adventure had first been planned.

I had been warned that the train journey from Sydney up to Brisbane would be long and cold, so I invested in half a bottle of Scotch for medicinal purposes. I certainly needed it. Talk about primitive! The seats were wooden and the 600-mile journey took from six o'clock in the evening until 10.30am the following morning. The average speed seemed to be about 40mph as we rumbled through the night, stopping at every remote station along the way. And it was every bit as cold as had been predicted. I hardly got a wink of sleep and by the time dawn broke, the whisky had long since disappeared.

Looking out of the window as we meandered up through New South Wales towards the Queensland border, I noticed that the mixture of forestry and farmland was gradually giving way to more and more sugar cane fields as we moved further north. The cane fields, which I had not seen before but which I was soon to encounter at much closer quarters, looked rather like acres of bamboo.

Vera was waiting to meet me on the platform at South Brisbane station. It was three months since we had seen one another and after a fond greeting we jumped straight into a taxi and headed for the flat in Kelvin Grove that she and Dot were sharing. They had both found quite good office jobs for themselves, Dot with an insurance company and Vera with the Brisbane equivalent of Britain's DVLC licensing authority.

I wasn't really supposed to stay in the flat – the landlord was a bit of a tyrant and deeply suspicious about unofficial tenants moving in – but a camp bed was put up in the living room on the understanding that I would only be there for a few days until I went on up to Murgon and the new job that Trish had helped to organise for me out in the bush.

Meanwhile, the girls showed me around Brisbane. Compared with Sydney, it was more like a large country town and I immediately felt much more at home there. You travelled mostly by tram and it was very easy to find your way around. We spent quite a lot of time with Trish's parents at their home on the north side of the city, had barbecues almost every day and enjoyed trips up to Bribie Island and along the Sunshine Coast to places with wonderfully strange-sounding names like Maloolaba and Maroochydore, then further on up to Coolum and Noosa. The beaches there were wonderful, often just as spectacular as Bondi but not nearly so crowded.

All too soon it was time to get on the coach up to Murgon and my job on the farm. Vera and I once again said our goodbyes and then I was off on a three-hour journey into the unknown and yet another new experience. Arriving at my destination, I was met off the coach by the farmer, Don Bishop. A real 'true blue' Aussie, he already owned two 'properties' and was about to buy a third, making some 2,000 acres in all. Land was incredibly cheap out there at the time – on the way out to his place he told me how an uncle of his had just bought 3,000 acres for a dollar-an-acre.

Don's main spread consisted of a homestead and six hundred acres where he kept a dairy herd of Jerseys – 'Daisy Cows', as he called them – and a load of pigs. The cows were primarily for cream production, while the skimmed milk was pumped down to the piggery, where Don had about four hundred bacon pigs as well as breeding stock. His second farm, up in the hills above Murgon, was for beef cattle and the third one that he had just bought would be used to expand this side of his business. I was already beginning to realise just how much work I had let myself in for.

After supper, I settled into my new quarters, a bunkhouse adjoining the main farmhouse building. It was all fairly basic. There were no fly screens on the windows and after a fitful night's sleep that was regularly disturbed by the menacing sound of dive-bombing mosquitoes, I awoke early the next morning to find that I was covered in so many bites that I looked as if I'd got chicken pox.

I didn't have much time to fret over that. Work started at 5.30am sharp, so that we could get the cows in for milking before the flies began to make life too uncomfortable. Don's wife brought out some tea and toast while we were doing the milking and when we'd finished that and had done all the clearing up, we then had to feed all the pigs before we could have our own breakfast, by which time it was about nine o'clock. However, the meal was worth waiting for. Out in the bush, the Aussie farmers always have a very substantial breakfast that usually includes steak and eggs or chops or bacon fritters – large pancakes filled with bacon.

Breakfast over, the daily routine would continue with mucking out down at the pigpens. While this was being done, the sows would be allowed to run out in a couple of paddocks where, every morning, the first job was to plough a couple of furrows to expose the wild potatoes or yams that grew there. The pigs loved this stuff and would get very excited as soon as they heard the tractor starting up.

I hadn't been there long when, one morning as we were working down at the piggery, I spotted a movement behind Don and was just in time to see a large snake disappear under a nogurabur bush. I alerted Don, who immediately looked very anxious and asked me what colour it was and what its markings were. He didn't usually swear much, but when I described what I'd seen his instant reaction was: "Shit! It's a brown! Go and get the rifle, quick."

I ran into the house and grabbed the gun out of the cupboard. I had never handled a rifle before, but I'd had plenty of experience with shotguns and air rifles so I knew what to do. By the time I got back down to the piggery, Don was still rooted to the spot, keeping a very nervous eye on the five-foot-long snake that was now starting to emerge from under the bush. Being a 'green' Pom, I didn't really appreciate the threat it posed.

"Shoot the bloody thing," shouted Don, who turned out to be much more frightened of snakes than I was. "It's deadly poisonous!"

I took aim and blew its head off with a single shot. Don was highly impressed.

"Strewth, Bernie! Where did you learn to shoot like that, mate?" he exclaimed.

I told him that I'd been shooting for years, adding nonchalantly that I'd actually won a big competition as a champion marksman on board the ship coming over! That was the first of many occasions in Australia when I proved that I deserved to have the letters BA after my name. Not so much Bachelor of Arts as Bullshit Artist! That was a useful qualification to have out there.

A few days later, Don announced that we would be going up to the farm he had just bought to do a bit of mustering. Could I ride a horse, he asked?

"Of course," I replied, despite the fact that the nearest I'd ever actually been to a horse was on the few occasions when I had been to watch my childhood girlfriend, Barbara Walker, riding in local gymkhanas back in Warwickshire. The next thing I knew, Don and I were loading a couple of horses into a truck, along with saddles, bridles and all the rest of the tack, plus a tucker box for our lunch.

The new property was up in the hills, about eight miles away from the main farm, and from then on we would go up there every three weeks or so to spray the herd for ticks and to do any weaning or cutting that was required. The cattle were a bit wild, being left there on their own for three weeks at a time, so rounding them up on horseback was quite an experience, especially for someone who had never ridden before! Somehow, I managed to avoid falling off, but, needless to say, I was so saddle sore after the first session that I could hardly walk the next day.

Apart from that, I rather enjoyed playing at being a cowboy. And the abundant wildlife out in the bush provided an added interest. Among other things, I saw my first wild turkeys. I was told that these timid birds made very good eating, although I never actually got to sample one myself as they were a protected species, with a two thousand dollar fine for anyone caught shooting them.

Within a few weeks, I'd met and made friends with quite a few of the locals in Murgon, but there wasn't an awful lot to do and I was itching to get back to the bright lights of Brisbane to see Vera and Dot. The chance came after I managed to buy an old Morris Oxford for A$70. It was wonderful to have my own transport at last and the very next weekend I set off after work on Friday and headed for the city. It was a journey of about one hundred-and-eighty miles, but with very little traffic on the long straight roads I found that I could do it in well under three hours. The main hazard you had to watch out for, especially after dark, was kangaroos asleep in the middle of the road. The tarmac retained the heat so they liked to stretch out there in the cool of the night. They were always getting hit – and a fully-grown roo could make quite a mess of a small car.

Arriving on the outskirts of Brisbane, I began to realise just how spread out the city is. Driving into the suburbs of Petrie and Lawnton, I thought I was almost there, only to find that I still had many miles to go before I reached the centre. After getting lost around Albion, I eventually found my way to Kelvin Grove where I got a warm welcome from Vera.

It was only a one-bedroom flat, and she and Dot each had a single bed. For the sake of appearances, just in case the landlord popped round unexpectedly, the camp bed was again put up in the living room. However, it remained unused. Sharing a single bed with Vera was a bit cramped, but we didn't mind that and Dot was very understanding, despite the fact that both she and Vera were good Catholic girls!

We spent this and the many weekends that followed either driving to the Sunshine Coast, north of Brisbane, or going south to the Gold

Coast. The beaches were fantastic and there were so many places to visit and explore – one way and another it made the bush seem rather boring.

Back at Murgon, I was in danger of getting stuck in the same sort of rut that I had been trapped in at home in England. The work was much the same, only the surroundings were different – and I was even starting to get used to them, too. From six in the morning until six at night I was hard at it, milking the cows, feeding the pigs and mucking out the pigpens. The bit I enjoyed most was being on horseback. I'd soon learned to ride quite well, holding the reins with one hand and cracking a whip with the other while cutting out cattle from the herd like a veteran of the Old West.

Coming up to Christmas and the New Year, it was the height of the Australian summer and getting hotter and hotter. I'd sometimes go riding bareback in the late afternoon and stop off at the main dam to cool off with a swim before milking. The flies were becoming more and more of a pest by this time of the year and we had to put a pink powder down around the milking bays in an effort to kill them off. The meat ants would then come and take them away. The meat ants' nests were raised mounds, with dozens of entrance holes, a bit like termites' nests. If you happened to disturb them they would come out in their dozens and attack you, not much fun when you were usually wearing nothing more than sandals and shorts.

Flying ants were another problem, especially on close, thundery nights when they would invade the house in vast swarms, attracted by the lights. They would end up everywhere and it would take a full can of spray to kill them off and then ages to clean up the mess left by the bodies. I was also starting to learn about some of Australia's other more unpleasant creepy-crawlies: snakes such as the brown, the king brown, the death adder, the red belly black, the taipan and the tiger snake and spiders like the funnel web, the redback and the trapdoor spider, so-called because it lives in a hole in the ground that has a little round lid made of mud under which it hides before raising the hatch and darting out to snatch unsuspecting victims. Australia is notorious for having more species of poisonous snakes and spiders than the rest of the world put together and I was to come up against quite a few of them during my time there. They never really bothered me that much and, even in the bush, I used to walk around most of the time in sandals, or 'thongs' as they are called out there.

Vera came up to Murgon for Christmas and stayed with me on the farm for a few days. I showed her around the places of interest in the area, although there wasn't really that much to see, certainly not compared to Brisbane. I sensed that she was not that sorry to leave and get back to the city. New Year's Eve was then spent with Don and his wife and as they were teetotal, I found myself toasting the start of 1967 in ginger beer!

It was now coming to the end of the summer and once again I was getting restless. I certainly had no intention of spending the next few years working long hours out in the bush for very little money. Twenty-eight dollars a week and my keep didn't seem much of a reward for what I was doing and, apart from that, the prospects were zero. Don had been a good boss and I had learned a lot from him and had also acclimatised myself to life in this strange new environment. But now I was eager to move on. I thanked him for everything, packed my bags and headed back to Brisbane for the next adventure.

Looking angelic at five (above left), and with my father, stepmother Wowey and baby sister Bridget (above right).

As a 15-year-old (on the left) with my cousin Jon Burnell and his dog on a rabbit-shooting trip at his home in Over Whitacre.

Wowey drives a tractor at Harbury, with my half-sister, Bridget, just visible on top of the hay bales.

Me and Barbara, on the right of the picture, with schoolfriends Ken Taylor and Maureen Harcourt on the playing field at Shipston High School.

Class picture at Shipston with me in the back row, third from the left.

(Above) Staff and students at Moreton Morrell agricultural college in 1963 (with me in the back row, sixth from the left).

(Below) a modern JCB Dancing Digger team in action.

With Roy Pool (leaning on the car) in Shipston – a right couple of likely lads!

(Below, left) My stepmother, Wowey, and (below, right) Barbara, with her scooter, shortly before Roy and I left for Australia in 1966.

The gang's all here! Aboard the Fairsea on the way out to Australia with (left to right) John, Roy, Mel, Vera, me, Trish, Gordon, Dot, Phil and Jimmy.

Roy and me, on the right, during our visit to the Pyramids.

At Parramatta Lake very
shortly after first arriving in
Sydney.

With Vera at
Southport Beach

Vera during a trip to
Surfers Paradise and
(left) looking
absolutely stunning
on our wedding day.

(Above) Vera and me with best man Harry Bennett and bridesmaid Dot.

(Below left) The full wedding party and (right) the happy couple.

CHAPTER 4

Love & Marriage

The main attraction of Brisbane as far as I was concerned was Vera. The relationship that had started on board the ship coming over had been growing steadily since then, despite the constant separations, and towards the end of my time in Murgon I had been living only for those weekends when I could jump into the car and drive down to see her. The days in between were spent counting the hours until my next visit.

Within weeks of me moving to Brisbane, we decided to get engaged. We went shopping together for a ring one Saturday afternoon, eventually choosing one with a setting that included a sapphire surrounded by twelve diamonds. That cost me about six weeks' wages, but the jeweller kindly agreed to let me pay it off in instalments. We celebrated with dinner at the Little Tokyo restaurant on the Sunday evening, but at one o'clock in the morning I then had to kiss Vera goodbye yet again and leave for work!

My first priority, on arriving in Brisbane, had obviously been to find employment. I actually applied again to join the police force – but I was still too short! After days of combing the situations vacant columns of the local newspaper I eventually managed to land a job on a lettuce farm just outside Brisbane at a place called Bunyaville. My new boss, Cliff Pepper, had eight of us working for him there on his twelve-acre smallholding. At A$60-a-week, the money wasn't bad, and accommodation was also provided in a prefab on site. This was a big advantage considering that there was no way I could move in permanently with Vera and Dot in their tiny flat in Kelvin Grove. However, the hours and conditions were, if anything, even worse than they had been in Murgon.

Our day began at three in the morning, when we would start cutting and packing the lettuces by the light of Tilley lamps before loading them onto a truck in time for Cliff to leave for the market at Rocklea by 6am. The mosquitoes would be extremely active during these early hours just before dawn and, despite liberal applications of industrial strength insect repellent, I was soon covered in bites.

Once Cliff had left for the market we would have two hours off for breakfast and would then spend the rest of the working day planting, weeding and spraying. The one bit of light relief amid this routine was when I was sent out in a truck to do the rounds of the racing stables at Ascot and Doomben, collecting horse manure for the lettuce beds!

The reason I got this particular job was that I was the only one of the workforce with an HGV licence. The way in which I had come by this was fairly typical of the laid-back Australian attitude to life. For a while, up in Murgon, I had been driving the farm lorries around on my English licence, but knew that I would have to get an Aussie one eventually. I had just taken a load of pigs to the abattoir in the cattle truck one day when I happened to be passing the local police station and decided to drop in to inquire about the formalities. The sergeant said he would be happy to take me for a test drive there and then, but had second thoughts when he wandered out and caught a whiff of the stinking cattle truck, still dripping with pig slurry.

"Tell you what, mate," he said, wrinkling his nose. "No need to go out. Why don't I just ask you a few questions?" He then asked me what the speed limit was?

"30mph in town and 60mph out in the bush," I guessed, not being absolutely sure. In fact, the limit was actually 35mph in town and unlimited in the bush, but the sergeant didn't seem too bothered.

"OK. That'll do," he said and proceeded to issue me with a licence on the spot.

Unfortunately, not every Aussie copper could be relied on to be quite so understanding. Racing back to Bunyaville in the early hours after my celebration dinner with Vera, hurrying to get there in time to start work punctually at 3am, I managed to get caught in a speed trap. That cost me another half-a-week's wages, something I could ill afford at the time. One way and another, it had been an expensive weekend!

Cliff was a good guy to work for and I also got on well with the rest of the team there. The only problem was Cliff's wife. She was a real tyrant, always taking the opportunity to boss us around whenever Cliff wasn't there. I became increasingly fed up with this until, one day, my patience snapped and I told her exactly where to stick her lettuce farm. When Cliff returned from the market he tried to smooth things over, but I couldn't resist telling him what I thought of the old dragon and left as soon as I got my pay.

Finding myself suddenly both jobless and homeless, I headed back to Kelvin Grove. By this time, however, the landlord was getting very awkward about me being there, so I had no option but to move to the south side of the river where so-called 'serviced rooms' could be rented very cheaply. For just A$9-a-week you got a bare, single room with a wash basin in one corner. There were facilities to make tea and coffee, but breakfast was not available, although you could pay extra to have sandwiches delivered to your room each morning. It was pretty grim, but I had no alternative until I could find myself another job.

After doing the rounds of local businesses for a day or two, I got taken on as a truck driver by a company called Red Comb that supplied animal feed for stock and poultry. They also had a hardware department. The transport manager, Eddie, asked me if I was familiar with the road layout in and around Brisbane and, calling on my BA qualification, I assured him that, of course, I did. I then got hopelessly lost on my first trip, but managed, somehow, to bluff my way out of trouble when I eventually found my way back to base.

The first truck I was given to drive was an ancient Dodge Kew with a five-speed crash box. Officially, we were only supposed to carry a five-ton load, but with the Dodge's long body you could actually get about eight on it. Most of the work involved going down to the docks on the Brisbane River to pick up supplies of soya or meat meal. The worst bit of the job was when you had to collect fish meal. This came in thin hessian sacks and you would end up getting covered in the stinking stuff. It was so disgusting that we got paid an extra twenty-cents-a-day for handling it. Thankfully, it wasn't too long before I got up-graded to a better truck, a Thames Trader, which was much cleaner and easier to drive. And having got to know my way around Brisbane, I was given a couple of regular delivery runs.

After a while I was then switched to the hardware department, where I was involved in transporting and installing bulk feed bins and big rainwater tanks to farms in the area. This was a two-man job and I had a regular mate working with me. The best thing about it was that it got us out of the city and into the bush.

On one occasion we found ourselves delivering a rainwater tank to an outlying farm at a time when it had been tipping it down with rain for hours. We turned off the main road onto the farm track, which became more and more flooded as we went along it until we got to a point where we just couldn't go any further. We then had what we thought was the brilliant idea of floating the tank the last couple of hundred yards to the farm. This worked fine, except that as the rain continued to bucket down, the track behind us became so badly flooded that we couldn't get the truck out again. By this time it was starting to get dark and the mozzies were coming out in force. In the end, we had to get the boss to send a tow truck to pull us out. We thought we had shown real initiative in delivering the tank by water, but we didn't get a very good reception when we eventually arrived back at the depot.

While all this was going on, Vera and I were spending our weekends exploring as much of the area as possible. We spent a lot of time either venturing up the Sunshine Coast or heading south down the Pacific Highway to Surfers Paradise. Here, even if you didn't have a surfboard, you could still have great fun body surfing. This entailed swimming out to sea and waiting for a big wave to come, then swimming like mad just in front of it. If you were lucky and timed it just right you would be carried all the way back to the beach. It was wonderfully exhilarating, but the power of those big Pacific rollers could often be quite frightening and if you got your timing even slightly wrong you would get bowled over and dragged along the bottom. The feeling then would be as if you were revolving in a vast tumble drier filled with water and lined with sandpaper and you would end up being hurled out onto the beach, covered in painful grazes.

One weekend we decided to visit Mount Tamborine. Located about forty minutes' drive inland from Surfers Paradise in what was once an area of dense sub-tropical rainforest, this 2000ft-high plateau is about five miles long by three miles wide and is renowned for its extremely colourful birdlife. Aptly-named Rainbow Lorikeets, red and green King Parrots, blue and yellow Pale Headed Rosellas and red and purple Eastern Rosellas are among the most spectacular. If you're lucky, you can also see bandicoots, possums, wallabies and even koala bears, while the croaks of various frogs combine with the birdsong to produce a real jungle soundtrack. If the beaches below are a paradise for surfers, then Mount Tamborine is a paradise for nature lovers.

On the way back, we came down to earth with a bang when the poor old Morris Oxford, which by now had done a fair few miles, hit a rock on the dirt road out in the middle of the bush, cracking the sump. With no engine, we coasted as far as we could down towards Boonah and then waited for another car to come along. As always happens out in the bush, the first person that came along stopped to help. Unfortunately, neither of us had a tow rope, but he had the bright idea of taking a length of wire out of a nearby fence to serve the purpose. He towed us back to Boonah, where we left the car at a garage, and then gave us a lift on to the railway station at Ipswich. We had to wait ages for the last train back to Brisbane, but the friendly station master made us some 'billy tea', which was very welcome. It was nearly midnight by the time we finally got home.

The garage fixed the car during the week and I went back the following weekend to pick it up. Sadly, it was never quite the same after that and so I traded it in for a second-hand Mini – a lot smaller but very economical.

I also changed my digs. I'd had more than enough of sandwiches, hamburgers and other take-away food and managed to find a much better place at Red Hill, the neighbouring suburb to Kelvin Grove. Just around the corner from Vera and Dot, the location was also very convenient for getting to work, close enough to walk and only a few stops on the tram if the weather was really bad. And at A$13-a-week for bed and breakfast, plus an evening meal and all my laundry done as well, it was very good value.

Meanwhile, the job at Red Comb was going well. I had been promoted to driving and operating the big bulk delivery trucks – no more lifting of heavy, smelly bags of fish and meat meal for me. The best truck in the depot was a brand new Ford, which had ten gears and a really comfortable cab, complete with air conditioning and various other extras. Coveted by all the drivers, this had actually been allocated to a chap called Ken Johnson, but Ken was a moody sort of bloke and after a blazing row with Eddie, the transport boss, he just walked out one day. Much to the envy of my colleagues, the Ford was handed over to me.

I started work each morning at 6am and would carry out two or three deliveries a day, depending on how far I had to go. Most of our customers were located either somewhere up the Sunshine Coast or down along the Gold Coast towards the border with New South Wales, although I did have the odd trip inland to the country area around Rosewood.

One of the things I particularly remember about Rosewood was that the pub there had the old-style swinging doors, just like the saloons in the Wild West. Because of the job, we never used to drink during the day, of course, but we would always meet up after work for a couple of 'coldies' in the local just around the corner from the depot. Jim Winch, the driver responsible for getting dispatches down to the railway station, had to get them down there by four o'clock in the afternoon at the latest. After that, he would be finished for the day and would retire to the 'railway pub' early. We didn't knock off until five, so poor old Jim would already be 'in the chair' by the time we arrived and always seemed to end up having to buy the first round.

I was really enjoying the job, which I was beginning to think would be for life. On days when Vera wasn't working I would often take her with me on the last afternoon delivery run, especially if it involved a trip down the Pacific Highway and along the Gold Coast. I always made sure I had my swimming gear in the glove compartment of the truck and on the way home, after making the delivery, I'd stop off at Surfers Paradise and have a swim. The boss often remarked on the fact that I looked surprisingly clean for someone who had just delivered a load of dusty chicken feed. I used to tell him that I had got caught in a rain shower, but I suspect he knew exactly what I was up to. As long as I got the job done on time, he wasn't bothered.

Vera and I were spending every spare moment together, enjoying idyllic weekends down on the beach, going to the discos out at Oxenford on Saturday nights and then driving back down to Surfers Paradise after midnight for a spot of skinny dipping, not very sensible given that the sea was often very rough and you couldn't really see what you were doing.

We would often go out as a foursome with Dot and her new boyfriend, Harry Bennett. Another £10 Pom, Harry came from somewhere in the north of England. He had also worked as a truck driver for a time before moving on to a nice clean job in the stock room of a local department store. He was a good lad, with a great sense of humour. The only problem was that he was well over six foot tall and didn't fit very comfortably into the back of the Mini when we all drove out to the beach.

It was now 1968 and as both Vera and I were settled in good jobs we decided to go ahead and get married. That had been in my mind ever since I'd paid that tanner to walk through the wishing arch in Cairo and made a silent wish that Vera would one day be my wife. The date was set for July 27th, two years to the day since we had arrived in Sydney at the end of the voyage from England. There was a lot to organise – church, cars, reception, food, drink, flowers, honeymoon and so on – and with no family around, we had to do everything ourselves.

Vera being Catholic, we had to go and see the father at the local RC church in Red Hill. He turned out to be a very strict and bigoted Catholic who, when he discovered that I wasn't a fully paid-up member of any religion, refused to marry us. This reduced Vera to tears, so I promptly told him where to stick his church! We thought at first that we would have to give up altogether on having a church wedding, but, happily, we then found a more friendly Catholic priest in a neighbouring suburb.

Half Irish and half New Zealander, Father McMullen was very easy-going, with a dry sense of humour and a bit of a twinkle in his eye, in every way the complete opposite to his cold, unbending colleague down the road. I couldn't resist taking the Mickey out of him about the fact that he happened to be living next door to a convent full of nuns and he took it all with a smile.

Having got his blessing, we went ahead with all the arrangements. On the big day, Vera was given away by Harry Ebdon, another of the friends we'd made on the ship coming over. A bricklayer by trade, Harry had settled with his wife just north of Brisbane and I'd worked for him as a labourer once or twice at weekends to make a bit of extra cash. Dot was a bridesmaid and Harry Bennett acted as my best man. Being so tall, Harry already looked rather awkward and uncomfortable in his penguin suit and when he then put on his top hat it made him appear even taller and more ungainly. I'm afraid we all had a bit of a giggle at his expense.

The girls, on the other hand, looked lovely. They arrived at the church in style in a Chevy Impala – a big, flashy American job that we had hired as a wedding car through a friend, for the princely sum of A$10. The ceremony went very smoothly and the reception afterwards was held back at the flat in Kelvin Grove. There were so many friends and workmates that we couldn't fit them all in and the party spilled out onto the lawn

It was a pity, obviously, that no family members from either side could be there. For me, there was a surprise when the old man sent a cheque for £25 as a wedding present. This was completely unexpected because although I had been writing to Wowey on a regular basis, I had not had any communication whatsoever with my father since the day I had walked out on him at Harbury.

For our honeymoon, Vera and I went up to the Great Barrier Reef, driving past Cairns as far as Port Douglas and covering a total distance of well over 2,500 miles during the fortnight we were away. Snorkelling out on the reef itself was one of the highlights for me and although Vera wasn't so keen on the actual snorkelling, a glass-bottomed boat enabled her to enjoy the underwater spectacle in comfort. Altogether, it was a memorable trip, the first of what were to be several Odysseys around Australia during the next few years.

Just before the wedding, Vera had announced the surprise news that she was expecting a baby. This was obviously going to change our lives. For a start, we would need to think in terms of more spacious accommodation. We rented a house in Bardon, another suburb not far from Kelvin Grove. This, again, was conveniently close to work and had the added advantage that there was enough space outside to park the truck if I finished late.

As the pregnancy progressed, Vera had to give up work and, with nothing much else to do, she started coming with me on my deliveries a lot more often. My boss, Eddie, didn't seem to mind at all as long as I loaded up first before going on to collect Vera.

It got to February 1969 and Vera was due any day. It was the middle of summer and the weather was hot and humid, which didn't make it any easier for her. After a few practice runs to the hospital, just a couple of miles down the road, we we were pretty well rehearsed. In the end, everything started happening at about three o'clock in the morning. In time-honoured fashion, I did my best to stay calm and not to panic while trying to manoeuvre a rather large Vera into our very small Mini. With no traffic around at that time in the morning we got to the hospital within minutes.

I wasn't allowed to be present for the birth – that still wasn't routine in those days, certainly not in Australia! – but at around ten-to-eight that morning I became the father of a lovely daughter. Louisa Anne weighed in at just over seven pounds. Back at work, all the truck drivers celebrated with me. Despite the tough reputation, they were a bunch of softies at heart. They even clubbed together to buy a present for the baby, which I thought was really nice of them.

Now that there were three of us, it was time to change the car again. The Mini wasn't really safe with a baby on board. As the paintwork wasn't too good, I waited until it was raining before going down to the local used car lot to trade it in, hoping that it wouldn't show quite so much. I replaced it with a Ford Falcon pick-up truck. This was much bigger altogether, with room in the back for a pushchair.

As a proud dad, I was now enjoying life to the full. The job was still going really well and by the time Lou was a few months old, Vera started bringing her along when she accompanied me on my trips, all three of us sitting up there in the cab together.

Before long, with a few dollars in the bank by now, we decided that it was time to have a place of our own instead of renting. Our next-door neighbour in Bardon happened to be an estate agent and he tipped us off about a plot of land at Burpengary, a suburb on the northern outskirts of Brisbane that had just come up for sale at a bargain price. I paid just A$1,300 for the five acre plot, on which I intended to build a house.

The ground was very rough and covered in scrub, which was why it was so cheap, but I set about clearing it by hand with an axe and a mattock. I spent every weekend there as well as every spare moment in the week when I could fiddle a couple of hours off work after completing a delivery ahead of schedule. During the weekends, Vera and I would often work there together, with Lou sitting in her pushchair, covered with a mozzie net.

We eventually got it cleared and lined up a local builder, who said he could build the house for A$7,500. We went along to the bank and arranged a loan and were all set to go ahead when our neighbour then advised us that the land would now be worth A$3,500 and that he had a prospective buyer. We couldn't resist the idea of such a quick and handsome profit and duly sold out.

It wasn't just the money. Our decision was also influenced by certain other factors that had combined to make us think again about whether we really wanted to settle down permanently in Brisbane. For one thing, the situation at work had changed slightly and I was not so sure I wanted to carry on there. At the same time, the council had decided to get rid of the city's lovely old trams, replacing them with buses. Apart from the fact that the trams had been such an attractive feature of Brisbane's everyday life – albeit sometimes rather inconvenient, when you got stuck behind them in your car or truck – the buses further spoilt the environment by noticeably filling the place with diesel fumes.

All this helped to remind us of why we had come to Australia in the first place. We had set out full of hope and ambition to see a bit of the world, maybe to make our fortunes, but, above all, to bring a bit of adventure into lives that had become humdrum back at home. We obviously had extra responsibilities now that we had got Lou, but that didn't mean that we had to forget all our dreams and settle for a suburban existence that was every bit as dull and routine in many ways as what we had left behind in England, except that it was lived out under blue skies and sunshine rather than grey clouds and drizzle.

After much discussion and a lot of enquiries we made up our minds to take to the road and to follow the sun and the seasonal work around Australia.

CHAPTER 5

On The Road

It was just before Christmas 1969 when we loaded eight-month-old Louisa and all our worldly belongings into the sixteen-foot Chesney caravan that we had bought with some of the proceeds from our land sale and headed off on the 1,000-mile journey down to Victoria for the start of the fruit-picking season.

We had plenty of time before the season got underway in January, so we took it easy along the coast road, meandering down through Queensland and New South Wales and stopping off for the night every hundred miles or so. This was a part of Australia I had only glimpsed fleetingly as I came up on the train three years earlier and I was keen to see more of it.

By now, Lou was starting to toddle and whenever we spotted a particularly nice beach we would pull over and take a break so that she could have a paddle and play in the sand. This also gave Vera and I a chance to relax, helping to ensure that the long trip became an enjoyable family experience.

It took us a while to adjust to caravan life and we suffered one or two small mishaps. On the second day, for instance, we left a large, open can of beetroot in the fridge but carelessly forgot to replace the pin that held the door closed. The next time we stopped we found, to our horror, that there was beetroot everywhere, mixed in with most of the other contents of the fridge.

This happened when we were just north of Sydney. We made a detour round the west side of the city and drove through Parramatta, so that I could show Vera the boarding house on O'Connell Street where Roy and I had been living when we first arrived. From what I could see, Sydney was expanding fast and had changed quite a lot even in the short space of time since I had last been there.

South of the city it was mostly sheep country, which wasn't awfully exciting, so we opted to make another detour inland in order to visit the Australian capital, Canberra. This turned out be very clean, tidy and well ordered, but also rather antiseptic and soul-less. Designed in a circle around Capital Hill, it had a maddening grid system of endless one-way streets that was fine until you missed your turning. Once that happened, it wasn't easy get back on track and we kept getting lost. We eventually managed to find the caravan park we were looking for and went off to have a closer look around.

Apart from Capital Hill, Parliament House, Government House and all the other administrative buildings, the most interesting feature by far was the National Museum. We spent nearly all day there, looking at exhibits that included the remains of the Japanese miniature two-man submarines that famously penetrated Sydney Harbour during World War II and actually fired a torpedo up Bondi Beach. We learned an enormous amount about Australian history, including some fascinating stuff about the early days of the penal colonies and the exploits of characters such as the outlaw Ned Kelly.

For us, it was amazing to think that in terms of European civilisation the country, in 1969, was still less than two hundred years old, Captain Cook having landed there to claim it for the British Crown only in 1770. Colonisation dated from 1788, when a fleet arrived with 1,500 settlers, half of them convicts. Up until then it had been a vast, mostly inhospitable wilderness, sparsely populated by isolated communities of Aborigines and Torres Strait islanders. We came away from the museum knowing an awful lot more about the country than when we went in.

From Canberra, we continued on down to the border with Victoria. Southern New South Wales was very hot and very dry. Inland, it was almost entirely sheep country, with many miles between each isolated farm – very different from the coastal areas of Queensland and northern New South Wales.

Once we got down past Wagga Wagga to Albury and Wodonga the scenery began to change. With the Murray River flowing through it, the area here was much greener, with a lot of fruit and vegetables being grown on land irrigated from the river. This was the first time we had seen crop-growing on this scale anywhere in Australia. On our first night there we stayed at a caravan park right on the banks of the Murray, where we suffered the extremely unpleasant experience of being introduced to the notorious Scots Grey. This fearsome type of mozzie is twice the normal size, with a bite to match. Unfortunately, as we were soon to find out, there were heaps of them where we were heading.

The next day was to be the last leg of our journey south for the time being. We arrived at Shepparton, about 100 miles north of Melbourne, in the afternoon and settled in at a caravan park that had its own lake. I soon found out that both the lake and the nearby Goulborn River, from which it was fed, contained some excellent fish, including trout, redfin and the famous Murray Cod. We were soon to sample all of these.

As it was the high season, the caravan park was pretty full. Shortly after we arrived, another couple, Derek Shadbolt and his wife, Joy, moved into the berth next to us. They, too, were £10 Poms, originally from Wales, and they had a son who was exactly the same age as Lou. Like us, they had decided to travel around doing seasonal work wherever they could find it and had spent the previous few weeks driving more than 2,500 miles across from Western Australia, where Derek had been working on the fishing boats north of Perth. Part of their journey had been through the Nullabor Plain, leaving the caravan covered in fine red dust, inside and out.

Once we had settled in, Derek and I immediately went out in search of jobs in the area. Bert, the caretaker at the caravan park, was extremely helpful in this respect and gave us the names of several local fruit farmers that he thought were likely to be hiring. I struck lucky with the first one I went to see, a chap called Phil Young. Phil sent all the fruit from his orchards to the local SPC cannery in Shepparton. He employed quite a few regulars who came back year after year, but was only too happy to take on some extra hands. I was to start on wages of three dollars-an-hour for the first few days, while I learned the ropes. After that, I would be paid the regular contract-picking rate of four dollars-a-bin, each bin measuring four foot square by about three foot deep.

Derek, meanwhile, decided that he didn't really fancy the hard work and the heat out in the orchard and opted instead for a job in the cannery, making wooden pallets and boxes for the fruit growers.

The following Monday, after a relaxing weekend that included a bit of trout fishing in the lake from a little aluminium boat that I borrowed from Bert, I reported for work at the orchard where I was first shown what to do by a couple of experienced pickers. John and Dez came from up around Mackay in Queensland, where they would spend the winter working in the sugar cane fields before coming south every year for the fruit picking season, living in so-called 'barracks' out in the orchards. Typically tough, wisecracking Aussies, they soon taught me the tricks of the trade.

We started off with the 'size picking' of pears, which involved picking only premium fruit of a certain size for SPC's top brands. This was obviously a much slower process than 'stripping', where you just took everything off together, and as a result it took longer to fill each bin and earn your four dollars. We made up for this by starting earlier, at about six o'clock in the morning, and working through until after five o'clock in the evening. We soon got onto stripping and then it was no problem to fill as many as ten bins a day. This was fantastic money, especially as we were working seven days a week. Even better, Phil had some sort of tax fiddle going whereby we worked half the week under our real name and the rest of the time under different names. This meant we got half our wages free of tax.

It was hard work and we certainly earned our money. For the first few days I was absolutely knackered by the time I got back to the caravan after lugging the large fruit-picking bag around all day. I was obviously out of condition, having spent the previous month either travelling or sitting around on the beach, but I soon got my fitness back and then, although the work was still tiring, it wasn't quite so exhausting.

When we'd finished with the pears, we moved on to the peaches. If I'd thought the itching bites of the Scots Grey mozzies were bad, the peaches turned out to have an equally irritating effect. We called them 'hairy Marys' because of the very fine hairs in which they were covered and which, as you picked them, got into your eyes, ears, nostrils and every joint in your arms. It was a horrible job, but the money was even better – six dollars-a-bin.

After the peaches, the picking season ended with the apples – mostly Jonathans and Granny Smiths. This was much cleaner work, but just as backbreaking, and it took us through until the end of March.

While I was out working, Vera looked after Lou, got on with the shopping and the cooking and spent time with the other young wives and mothers on the site. Most of the families there were doing the same as us, with all the husbands working out in the orchards, so it soon became rather like any other small community. I managed to take a few weekends off in between picking the different crops at the orchard. Derek, meanwhile, was working night shifts and weekends for the extra money, so Vera and I would often take his wife and son out with us to explore the surrounding area. This was mostly rather flat and relatively uninteresting, although there were some nice picnic spots along the banks of the Goulborn River, which was where we ended up most of the time. I liked to do a bit of fishing and anything I caught would be barbecued for tea. Murray Cod was the best to eat, while redfin was also quite tasty, although so tough-skinned that you had to skin them with a pair of pliers!

Once the fruit season was over it was time to move on down to Ballarat, about 120 miles south of Shepparton, for the spud picking. When we arrived the rain was tipping down and it continued almost non-stop for over a week. I started enquiring about a job, but the ground was far too wet to get onto with the machinery so absolutely nothing was happening. After a further few days of heavy rain we eventually gave up and decided to head back to Queensland and the sunshine. Derek and Joy, who had accompanied us down to Ballarat, thought they would do the same. They were keen to explore the whole of the East Coast while we were more interested in taking an inland route, having already seen much of the coast. We therefore arranged to go our own separate ways, but agreed to meet up again in Mackay, 500 miles north of Brisbane.

We set off back to Albury, and from there headed out into the bush to Wagga Wagga, Junee and Coatamundra, on to Cowra and Orange and then east towards Tamworth. This all took several days and up in the Great Dividing Range of mountains it was getting colder and colder, especially at night, so that we were soon longing desperately for the warmth and sunshine of Queensland. The coldest places of all were Tenterfield and Warwick, up near the border between New South Wales and Queesland. We didn't hang around there too long but hurried down to the coast just north of Brisbane where our spirits quickly rose, along with the temperature.

Having made a fair bit of money down south, we had decided to treat ourselves to a few days' holiday up around Mackay. It was now May and the cane season would soon be starting there, with plenty of opportunity for work. In the meantime, we thought we would take it easy for while, exploring a bit more of the area around Cairns, where we had spent our honeymoon. We did a bit of sightseeing but spent most of our time on the beach with Lou, who enjoyed this as much as we did. We then found a really nice caravan park just south of Mackay at a place called Baker's Creek. The surrounding area was very tropical, with some beautiful gardens and, right behind the park, a banana plantation. We installed ourselves there and soon discovered that by taking the hatch off the caravan we could actually reach out and scrump a few bananas whenever the owner wasn't around.

All too soon, it was once again time to look for employment. I was told that you could get good money cane cutting, so I lined up a job on a farm just a couple of miles down the road. My first task there was to cut the young canes from the nursery beds, ready for planting out in the main fields. This was a labour-intensive process that involved cutting the canes and then stripping the dead leaves away using a special tool with a V-shaped blade before topping and tailing them with a machete-like knife and loading them onto trailer to be taken to the planting area. Here they would simply be stuck in the ground to root themselves and develop into full-grown plants.

I lasted just three weeks and three days in that job before jacking it in, by which time both my hands were covered in huge blisters. On top of that, the cane produced a similar 'hairy Mary' irritant to that which came off the peaches down in Shepparton, while the mozzies were just as bad as they had been on the fruit farms in Victoria. At least I didn't get bitten by one of the many snakes that lurked in the cane fields! Poisonous cane toads were also a major nuisance, so thick on the ground at times that you had to kick them out of the way just to clear a path as you walked. Although harmless to humans, they excreted poison from a sac on the back of the neck as a defence against attack and this was powerful enough to kill a dog or other predators.

While I was taking a week off to allow my blistered hands to heal, Vera came up with the slightly startling news that she was expecting again. She was actually three months pregnant, which meant that there was still plenty of time before we had to start thinking about making it back down to Brisbane for the birth. Meanwhile, the local cottage hospital in Mackay was able to look after all the various pre-natal check-ups, assuring us that everything was going smoothly.

Having recovered from the rather unpleasant experience of working in the cane fields, I decided to start looking around for something a bit different and before too long managed to land a job in the construction industry, with a company that was putting in a new sewerage system at Sarina, about twenty miles away. At that time most Aussie communities, especially those out in the bush, were still on septic tanks, with just a 'dunny' out in the back yard, but mains drainage was gradually spreading out from the towns. Apart from the fact that the money was good, this was also an opportunity for me to learn new skills.

I soon got the hang of it, so much so that I was very quickly promoted from general labourer to pipe layer, in charge of my own gang. I was working long hours, six days a week, but at least I was able to spend every Sunday with Vera and Lou, usually on the beach. Although it was winter, the weather was never really that bad. There were still plenty of warm days when we could sit on the sand and sunbathe and as well as paddling and building sand castles with Lou, we would also collect shells and sometimes even pick up coconuts, which were plentiful on the beaches north of Mackay.

By the middle of the October, however, it was time to head back to

Brisbane. Having settled the family into a caravan park on the northern side of the city, I managed to find a job similar to the one I had been doing up in Mackay, again installing new sewerage systems, this time at Sandgate, about fifteen miles outside Brisbane. The company was run by two Irishmen who, by some extraordinary coincidence, were both named Patrick Fitzgerald, although they were not related. It was all very confusing. To make matters even worse, the foreman was also called 'Paddy'.

They turned out to be a great gang to work for – and to play with, too, as long as you had the constitution for it. We started early, at 6am, and knocked off at four o'clock in the afternoon, whereupon the three Paddies would head straight for the pub "to wash the dust down". Quite often, they would then stay there for the rest of the evening. I would join them for a couple of beers, but, quite apart from the fact that I couldn't keep pace with them as far as the drinking was concerned, I preferred to spend as much time as possible with the family – especially as I was now working seven days a week.

I had been promoted from pipe layer to head of restoration, which entailed everything from erecting wooden fences to laying concrete paths and any other odd construction jobs that needed doing. Then, just as things were going really well, I went down with a very bad case of gastro-enteritis and spent the best part of two weeks sitting in the dunny back at the caravan park. That wasn't much fun. And to make matters worse, we had a spell of monsoon weather at the same time. Being next to a creek, the caravan park was soon flooded and we were left paddling around everywhere in six inches of water.

As the arrival of the new baby was now imminent, I parked the car up near the main gate to make sure that we didn't find ourselves stuck in the mud in the event that we needed to make an emergency dash to the hospital. This turned out to have been a wise precaution because, sure enough, things started happening the very next afternoon, right in the middle of another heavy downpour. Happily, everything went very smoothly and Tiffany arrived that evening, without any complications.

With a larger family, we now needed a bigger caravan. I traded in the sixteen-foot Chesney for a twenty-two-foot, six-berth Millard.

Along with the brand new annexe attachment that I also bought, this gave us a lot of extra space and helped to make life much more comfortable. At the same time, I swapped the pick-up for a more powerful Falcon station wagon.

Having recovered from my illness, I was now back working with the Irishmen, but knew that my days with them were numbered. Vera and I were already planning a second season of fruit-picking down at Shepparton, where I knew that a man with my experience could earn as much as A\$240-a-week, nearly twice what I was getting in the construction business. I quit my job with the Paddies just before Christmas and we headed south again.

Being seasoned travellers by this time, we knew exactly where we wanted to go and where to find the best places were to stop overnight. We set off at the crack of dawn, so as to get clear of Brisbane and the Gold Coast before the roads got too busy. Once we had crossed the border into New South Wales we took our time, stopping off at places such as Coffs Harbour, Port Macquarie and Taree that we had missed on the first trip and exploring every small beach as far down as Newcastle, just north of Sydney.

There was a shortage of work in all these coastal towns, but we knew that there would be rich pickings awaiting us down in Victoria so we pressed on, getting off to an early start and driving about 200 miles each day before looking around for a decent park for the night.

Except in some of the smaller one-horse towns, most of the parks along the way had excellent facilities. The thing you really looked forward to after a day's driving was a nice hot shower. You could also do all your washing, hang it out in the sun in the late afternoon and have it dry by suppertime. We would do most of our food shopping in the bigger towns as we passed through, so that we always had a constant supply in the caravan. And all along the coast there were roadside stalls selling fruit and vegetables. The kids were no problem. Tiff was only a few months old, so she slept most of the time, while Lou, who was just three, was always very good. There was plenty for her to see and we made sure we stopped at regular intervals, usually somewhere near a beach.

On reaching Shepparton, we went straight to the same caravan park where we had stayed the previous year, although now that we had two small children to look after we chose a different spot, a little further away from the lake, for safety's sake.

Unfortunately, because we were a little later arriving this time, all the picking jobs with Phil had already gone. However, it didn't take me long to fix myself up with something at an orchard just down the road that was run by two brothers, Merv and Bill. As bosses, they turned out to be just as good to work for as Phil. They had barrack accommodation for their pickers and as nobody else was staying there at the time we were invited to park the caravan there and make use of the shower and toilet facilities. This was an ideal set-up in every way. Apart from the convenience, it meant I didn't have to spend money on petrol getting to work and didn't have to live on sandwiches for lunch. There was also the great advantage of being closer to the family.

During the next few weeks I became very friendly with one of the other pickers, an ex-cane farmer from Queensland, called Norm. He and his wife had no less than six kids, the whole family living in a caravan about the same size as ours. I asked him how he managed to fit them all in and he replied, deadpan: "Easy, mate. I just wait until a few of them have fallen asleep and then stand them up in the corner!"

Because the older kids were going to school locally, he decided to stay up at the caravan park rather than moving down to the barracks, but Vera and I saw quite a lot of them during the time we were there. He and I chose to pick together because we worked at much the same pace. He told me how he had fallen on bad times and had been forced to give up the cane farm. Before opting for seasonal picking work he had done a bit of gold prospecting and had even found a few nuggets. The only problem was, they were on someone else's property!

He sold me his old .303 rifle. He reckoned it wasn't safe to travel out in the bush without some protection. Fortunately, I never had any trouble and never needed to use it, but I did feel a bit more secure in the knowledge that I had it there, stuck under the car seat – especially on those occasions when we stopped miles from anywhere for a picnic lunch and a cup of tea.

As the picking season drew to a close in March and it started getting colder, Norm and his family decided to head back to Queensland for the winter, but I opted to stay on for the pruning season. This started as soon as the leaves had fallen. Merv and Bill showed me how it was done and it didn't take me long to get the hang of it. We had to wait each morning until the frost had cleared and then worked like mad for the rest of the day. You got paid by the tree and could earn fifty dollars a day, which was even better than picking. Your earnings slowed down a bit when you got into the bigger trees and had to spend time going up and down ladders, but it was still good money. The only trouble was that you ended up with aching wrists and blistered hands from using secateurs all day long.

It was now getting into the middle of winter in Victoria and becoming much too cold for our liking, having being spoiled by the warmer Queensland climate. We decided to move on, but in a different direction this time. We'd never been further west than Melbourne and thought we might go on as far as Adelaide and the winelands of South Australia, where we had heard there were good jobs to be had in the vineyards.

Again, we took our time, travelling in short stages. We set off north through Kerang and did about 125 miles on the first day, stopping for the night at Swan Hill, back on the Murray River. We found a park on the banks of the river and I went fishing, intent on landing a Murray Cod for supper. Using a spinner or a floppy, you could always guarantee at least one four or five-pounder, which was all you needed for a decent meal.

Our next two stops were at Mildura and Renmark. Big country towns out in the bush, they weren't very exciting and as it was pretty chilly that far inland we began to wonder what we were letting ourselves in. It wasn't until we got to Tanunda and the Barossa Valley, just north of Adelaide, that things began to change for the better. This was the best wine country in South Australia, although it has to be said that the Aussie wine back in those days was pretty basic stuff, nothing like as good as it is today. The cheaper ones could leave you with a very bad head the next day. As it happened, we weren't great wine drinkers, so we carried on down the valley to Adelaide.

After carefully studying our map, we had picked out what seemed like a suitable caravan site just to the south of the city, but were unprepared for the steep hills leading down to it. This was not the ideal moment to discover suddenly that there was something seriously wrong with the car's brakes! Even using the air brakes on the caravan, I couldn't stop and we sailed straight on past the entrance to the park. God knows what would have happened if we had come upon an intersection, a set of traffic lights or some other emergency. As it was, the road was clear and we eventually rolled safely to a halt. I turned round and went back up the hill and into the park very slowly. Once we were settled there, I had a look and soon found the problem; one of the brake cylinders was leaking oil onto the brake shoes. Luckily, there was a garage nearby where I managed to get some new seals and made the necessary repairs.

First thing the next morning I was out job-hunting once again. There was nothing available in the vineyards or orchards at that time of year, but I eventually got work in the Chrysler car factory a couple of miles away from the caravan park. Chrysler Australia was about to launch two new models and the factory was operating six days-a-week to meet demand, so jobs were plentiful.

With a few days to spare before I started there the following Monday, we set out to explore the area and to see if we could find a more attractive caravan park than the one we were in. After taking a look around, we decided to move down to Christie's Beach, a few miles south of the city. Not only was the park there very close to the beach itself, but the shopping centre was also within walking distance, perfect for Vera and the kids.

My first job at Chrysler turned out to be boring in the extreme. I was put on the assembly line, setting and adjusting doors, and I did that virtually non-stop for ten hours a day, Monday to Friday, and for eight hours on Saturdays. After a couple of months I started to get very tired of this routine. The company then brought out a new range of executive cars that came complete with electric windows, seats and aerials. These extras couldn't easily be installed on the main assembly line so the cars had to be sent to a separate shop to be finished off. I had just suffered a hernia – a common complaint among those doing my job, because of the weight of the doors and the awkward angle at which you had to manhandle them during the assembly process – so I was able to get myself moved to this new department where the work was much easier and more interesting.

Working with me on the twenty-man team was yet another £10 Pom. Alex came from the north of England and, like me, he had married an English girl whom he had met on the way out. Also like me, he had had numerous jobs, including a spell as a truck driver. He and his wife lived just around the corner from us at Port Noarlunga and we saw quite a lot of them. In fact, I saw rather more of his wife than I really should have done since Alex, whose hobby was black-and-white photography, used to take pictures of her with not a lot on. He developed them himself and would then show off to me with great pride. I thought that was a bit odd, but it was certainly more interesting than having to look at somebody's holiday snaps!

Meanwhile, Vera had once again surprised me with the news that I was going to be a dad for the third time. As things would definitely be getting a bit cramped in the caravan, we decided to buy a house not far from where Alex and his wife were in Port Noarlunga. Apart from anything else, the strong winds down on the beach had nearly blown the annexe right off our van on one occasion, so it seemed more sensible all round to be in a house a little further away from the seafront.

There was a house-building boom in the area at the time and we soon found a very nice Mediterranean-style villa with three bedrooms for which we paid about twelve thousand dollars. Located just a few minutes walk from the beach, with a large garden back and front for the kids to play in, it perfectly fitted our requirements.

With a steady job, a growing family, a permanent home and a hefty mortgage, there now seemed every chance that I might be about to settle down for good. But that was not to be.

CHAPTER 6

The End of the Road

No sooner had we settled into our new home than Chrysler re-organised their production line and announced cutbacks that meant I was suddenly reduced to working only five days a week. The resulting drop in income couldn't have come at a worse time, as I had been forced to take out a double mortgage in order to finance the purchase of the house and the furniture to go in it.

To make ends meet, I had to take on a second job, working weekends at a farm just south of Port Noarlunga, a smallholding that was mainly into egg production but where they also grew vegetables. This was ideal. Not only was I able to supplement my wages with free eggs and all the vegetables I wanted, but the hours involved meant that I was still able to spend time with the kids down at the beach on Sunday afternoons. Now that Lou, in particular, was getting a lot more mobile, we had to be especially careful because the sea was very rough at times and even when you were paddling in the shallows you had to keep an eye out for the occasional big wave that could easily knock you off your feet. As for swimming, we'd been put off by the sharks that we'd seen cruising around just offshore. While we were still living on the caravan site down near the seafront, we used to sit out in the evenings and watch them for hours.

With the work at Chrysler gradually drying up altogether, I realised there was no future there and started looking around for something else. At that point I had a stroke of luck. My friend Alex had already left Chrysler to go house painting and after I had run through my usual BA routine, claiming to be an experienced painter and decorator, his boss offered me a job as well. The work, which was all conveniently local, was actually much more interesting than working in the factory and quite well paid. And with the paint left over from various jobs, I was able to redecorate the whole of my own house.

Vera was now due at any moment and, not being in any medical scheme, we had to pay all the hospital expenses, which added to the financial pressure. When the time came, I took a day off work and drove Vera to the maternity wing while a friend's wife looked after Lou and Tiff. This time the birth wasn't quite as easy as on the two previous occasions and Kerri only finally arrived after five or six hours' hard labour. Nevertheless, mother and baby were back home the next day.

No sooner had they come out of hospital than it was my turn to go in. My hernia had been causing me a lot of discomfort and even though I had already left Chrysler, the Union there kindly arranged for me to have the necessary operation done at a hospital in McLaren Vale, a small bush town south of Adelaide. I decided that while I was in there I might as well have 'the snip' at the same time. With three little ones and two mortgages, I didn't want to risk straining my finances any further.

I was in for nearly a week, altogether. The day before I was discharged an Aborigine nurse came to take the stitches out and rather botched what should have been a fairly simple, straightforward procedure. It was extremely painful and I made almost as much noise as Vera had made when she was in the final stages of labour, while the unfortunate nurse learned an awful lot of very colourful truck drivers' language in a very short space of time.

I returned home to find that things had gone from bad to worse on the work front. It turned out that while I had been laid up Alex had quietly been creeping round the boss and had somehow managed to get the foreman's job. He then decided that he didn't need me any more, so after a few choice words he was told exactly where to stick his brushes! I heard later that the firm had gone bust shortly afterwards and that Alex had lost his job and had ended up having to go back to truck driving. In the circumstances, I didn't feel too sorry for him.

Meanwhile, I had fixed myself up with something completely different down at the meat works in Noarlunga. It wasn't the sort of job for which you had a proper interview; you simply turned up at the factory gate, and if there was anything going you would get taken on. It was also rather a messy business and the environment in certain areas of the factory was not for the squeamish. However, I actually quite enjoyed it. Having worked on farms for years, and thanks also to my training at agricultural college, I knew quite a bit about animal parts.

I was allocated to the offal department, which, as you might imagine, was probably the least pleasant place in the whole establishment in which to work. Even that didn't bother me too much. In fact, the worst thing about it as far as I was concerned was that it was staffed almost entirely by a group of extremely coarse female workers whose foul language, filthy jokes and crude banter were enough to make a naval stoker blush!

Apart from me, the only other men working in the department were the foreman, Burt Taylor, a Brit who came originally from somewhere up in Lancashire, and a young lad called Wolfgang Keibet, who had emigrated from Germany with his parents some years previously. Wolfgang and I got on well right from the start. He was very keen on fishing, particularly shark fishing, which he did mostly at night. I soon started going with him and while I was content to catch smaller fish off the jetty, Wolfgang, who was all of fifteen stone, used his size and strength to haul in the much bigger ones, some of them up to six foot long. He would sell them to the local fishmongers who, in turn, supplied them to fast food restaurants for 'flake and hake', the popular Aussie fast food equivalent of fish 'n' chips.

We also spent quite a few nights fishing for brim down at Victor Harbour. Brim, the Australian equivalent of bream, are tricky fish to catch, but they make very good eating. Wolf showed me a place where you could drive right up to the riverside and sit fishing just in front of the car. This was very handy as Vera and the kids would come down with me some nights to watch. When the girls got tired they would simply curl up and fall asleep under blankets in the back of the station wagon.

The job at the meat factory was going very well by this time and I was promoted to despatch clerk in the department. Much to Burt's annoyance, I was also appointed Union rep in the department. The women were always complaining bitterly – and in typically robust terms – about how badly over-worked they were. In all fairness, their complaints were often quite justified, especially as some of the jobs they had to do were pretty disgusting, and so I regularly found myself having to go into the office to have it out with Burt on their behalf.

I then heard about a meat inspectors' course that was about to start at the local college of further education, with the head inspector at the factory as the main lecturer. As well as Wolfgang, I had also got friendly with a chap called Ron Gordon, who was working in the boning department, and he and I decided to enrol for the course together, attracted by the prospect of being able to earn very good money once we had qualified, with the added perk that a house would be provided in whatever part of the country we were sent to work.

We started the part-time course in the February of 1973. I found it quite easy to start with as I had done quite a lot of the same study at agricultural college back in England. Ron, who had never done anything like this before, found it more difficult, but with me helping him along he soon learned all about the blood, bones and every other body part of the various different animals. We even arranged to spend a few days working in the condemned room at the factory, where all the rejected meat and organs went for processing into meat meal, just so that we could gain valuable first hand experience about all the nasties that could turn up in the meat and what to look out for. This entailed learning a lot of very long and complicated technical names.

It was coming up to Easter when Vera suddenly got a letter from her mother back in England saying that she was about to be kicked out of her home in Cheshire by the local council, who were planning to knock the house down to make way for a new by-pass. Her mum had only seen photos of the kids so we decided that it would be a good idea for Vera to fly back in an effort to help sort things out, taking the girls with her. The tickets were booked and I waved them off from Adelaide airport. They were only going to be away for six weeks or so, but I knew that I was going to miss them.

Faced with the unexpected expense of the trip, I took out a further loan and started looking around for yet another extra job to help pay it off. In addition to my day job at the meat factory and my weekend job at the farm, I now took on a cleaning job in the local supermarket, working three hours a night, six days a week. And, in between, I had to find time to do all the homework for the inspectors' course. Despite the extra work, I managed to do very well in the exams at the end of the first term. Of the twenty-seven who had started the course, nine had either failed or dropped out, leaving eighteen of us, including Ron, to carry on for the second term.

I then had an urgent phone call from England to say that Vera's mum had lost the house and that although she had been fixed up with alternative council accommodation, there was no room there for Vera and the kids and nowhere else for them to stay. On top of that, the worry of it all seemed to have sent Vera's mum round the bend, but as there was nothing much more that Vera could do, she had decided to come back straightaway. We had bought only one-way tickets, because we weren't sure exactly how long they were likely to be staying, so there was then a mad scramble to get some money to the UK so that the return flights could be booked.

I took time off from the meat factory on the day they were due back and set off early that morning to pick them up from the airport, leaving myself plenty of time, or so I thought. But, sure enough, I then ran into major road works on the way and was still stuck in a traffic jam when I actually saw the plane fly in overhead. By the time I got there, the four of them had already cleared customs and immigration and were sitting there on their suitcases, waiting for me and looking very tired. After a fond re-union, it was out to the car and off back home.

The kids very soon recovered and couldn't wait to get down to the beach again. They hadn't enjoyed the cold, damp weather back in England. As for Vera and I, there was so much to talk about that we sat up until very late, catching up on all the latest news. Then it was into bed – and no worries about baby number four coming along!

Although autumn was now approaching, it was still warm enough to sit on the beach all day when we had the time, which, in my case, was not that often. I would join the others whenever I had an hour or two between jobs. Sometimes, Ron and his wife would also come along with their two boys. Ron had spent time in the Navy, during which he had learned to dive, and this had remained a hobby. He brought all his gear down to the beach one afternoon and invited me to accompany him on a dive. Remembering the sharks, I was a bit dubious at first but finally agreed.

Ron was very familiar with the reef just out from the south end of the beach and suggested we should start there. We got kitted up and he handed me a knife to strap to my leg, just in case. I must admit that I was quite nervous as we swam out, but once we got to the reef and started looking around it was absolutely fantastic and I was too interested in what there was to see down there to worry about anything else. As it happens, there were one or two small sharks swimming around, but they never bothered us.

I had been snorkelling once before, up in North Queensland, where the things you really had to watch out for were box jellyfish and stonefish. The pale blue, cube-shaped box jellyfish, with its three-metre tentacles, is one of the deadliest and most poisonous creatures to be found anywhere in the world, killing more people in Australia than sharks, snakes or crocodiles. You are said to have virtually no chance of surviving its sting, the pain of which is so excruciating that most victims go into shock and drown before they can even reach the shore. Anyone who is not immediately treated with anti-venom will almost certainly be dead within two or three minutes. The stonefish, which has thirteen highly poisonous spines along its back, also delivers a very painful sting although this is not usually fatal. What with one thing and another, you have to keep your eyes open and your wits about you when you go for a dip in Aussie. No wonder, then, that most people prefer to stick to the beach!

With house prices booming, we decided to cash in on our place in Port Noarlunga in favour of a rented house a bit further down the coast. This turned out to be a very bad move as the house was made of asbestos and got freezing cold at night. What's more, the nearby beach included a nudist section so we had to be careful where we took the kids.

We very quickly moved on again to another rented property just down the road from the meat factory. This place had a very large garden, with plenty of room to grow vegetables and a secure back yard and lawn for the children. As an added bonus, there was a river running just across the road and what with the fish that I regularly managed to catch there, plus the cheap meat and bacon I could get from work, it didn't cost a lot to feed the family.

Thanks to the profit from the sale of the Port Noarlunga house we now had a few thousand dollars in the bank and that, along with the availability of a lot more overtime at the meat factory, meant that I was able to quit my part time jobs at the farm and the supermarket. This was a relief since I was now finding that I had to work even harder on my studies for the meat inspection course. It also gave me the opportunity to spend more with the family at weekends.

As well as the beach, we started going down to Victor Harbour, where the fishing was especially good. On one trip down there we stopped off at a local creek we had previously spotted and liked the look of. I got the trout rod out and had a quick go with a spinner and, much to my surprise, almost immediately hooked a beautiful big rainbow trout. We cleaned and gutted it and found when we got it home that it weighed nearly five pounds. Stuffed and baked on the barbecue, it made wonderful eating. I fished that creek again many times after that but never managed to catch anything quite as big.

The other place where I enjoyed some great fishing was at a holiday cottage down the coast that was owned by one of Wolf's mates and which he allowed us to borrow from time to time when he wasn't using it himself. It was located right down on the beach and I usually managed to land enough fish each day to keep the whole family fed, cooking the day's catch on the barbecue for supper.

With the girls growing up, we then invested in another small caravan for holidays and weekends away, and when the meat factory's annual two-week holiday came up we decided to go off and explore the rest of South Australia.

We first headed north out of Adelaide, up to Port Pirie and on to Port Augusta on the Spencer Gulf. Port Pirie is very much an industrial town and not a place to linger in, while Port Augusta is the gateway to the Great Victoria Desert, a couple of hundred miles north, and to the Nullarbor Plain in the west. We travelled north towards the desert town of Coober Pedy for a while to see what it was like and found dry, arid country with dirt roads covered in what was called 'bulldust'. Very fine, like pepper, this would rise in a cloud behind you, completely obliterating the view both for anyone following behind you and anyone approaching from the opposite direction.

We turned round at that point and headed back to Port Augusta and then down the other side of the Spencer Gulf, through the ship-building town of Whyalla to Port Lincoln, where tuna fishing is the main industry. People had told us how nice it was, but we were not that impressed with the town itself when we got there and didn't hang around too long. Instead, we re-traced our steps and eventually settled in a caravan park a few miles up the coast.

The beaches on the gulf were sandy and very safe for the kids and we also had a lot of fun fishing off the jetty for Tommy Ruff. This entailed putting six or seven hooks on one line, baited with dough. A scattering of breadcrumbs would then cause a feeding frenzy and you could guarantee at least four or five fish every time you cast out. They were only the size of sardines, but were perfect for the barbecue. And the girls loved the fact that they were so easy to catch, with no long, boring waits for a bite.

All too soon, it was time to pack up and head for home. With the holiday over, I had to get back to work while at the same time revising hard in preparation for the meat inspection course's end-of-year exams. Parked back at the house, the caravan was the ideal place in which to study, away from the noise of the children. Time was running out and Ron and I spent most evenings shut away there, going over the first year's work.

The dreaded day soon arrived. Ron picked me up in his car and after a large scotch to settle our nerves it was off to the college and the exam room. Several more people had dropped out of the course in the previous few months and there were now only twelve of the original twenty-seven left. The exam lasted three hours and was not that easy, involving a lot of very technical stuff. At the end, Ron and I breathed sighs of relief and headed home for another large scotch or

With daughter Louisa on the beach during
our travels in 1970.

Vera with Louisa during a trip to Mackay.

Louisa with Tiff (on the rocker), in the
garden at Port Noarlunga.

On the road in New South Wales with the
Millard caravan and the big Falcon estate
car.

Our first permanent home in Port
Noarlunga, South Australia.

A death adder, one of the more unpleasant creepy crawlies that you have to look out for in Australia.

Enjoying a spot of sea fishing in 1967 at Noosa Head, a favourite spot north of Gympie.

Ted, in the trench, doing a bit of hand-mining in Sapphire.

(Below) the first cut on a new claim that I bought after going into business on my own. It yielded $A13,000 worth of stones in just eleven days – seriously good paydirt!

Mining operations in full swing on my Sapphire claims. The bulldozers, having first made the 'cuts', would heap up the 'dirt' (below, left).

This would then go through a series of washing and sifting process that would separate the gemstones from the sand, gravel, clay and ironstone.

(Above) The White House, our home in Sapphire that I built myself and that was regarded as the best house in the area.

(Left) My first attempt at housebuilding, the one I put up for Ted and Edna.

A typical gemfield view in Sapphire.

Tiff and Penny at Fairbairn Dam (above), on the beach at Surfers Paradise (left) and on the farm at Gympie. In each case, Tiff is on the left of the picture.

Barbecueing crabs with Ted and Edna's son John, who worked for me on the claims.

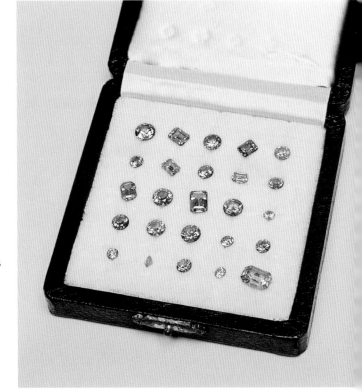

Part of the collection of sapphires that I mined and had cut for myself. At one time only blue corundum qualified as a sapphire, but although the blues still tend to be the most highly valued, the colours actually range through all shades of blue, green, yellow, pink and orange. Rarest and most valuable are gold sapphires.

two. We then had to wait more than a week for the papers to be marked and the results to be announced. People had been doing the same course elsewhere in the state, at centres in Mt Gambier and also north of Adelaide. Much to my amazement, I scored 100% and was named top student in the whole of South Australia. Unfortunately, there was no prize – just hearty congratulations from my tutor. Ron didn't do quite so well, but managed to get through to the second year of the course with a good pass.

During the following few weeks, work at the meat factory seemed to slow right down. Although Vera and I liked the area around Noarlunga, we still preferred Queensland and so I wrote to enquire about similar work back there and the possibility of completing the second year of the inspectors' course up in Toowoomba, where there were a couple of large meat factories. On being told that this would be no problem and that a job was pretty much guaranteed, we decided to make the move back.

We had quite a lot of furniture to take with us, so we sold the car and bought a small truck with which to tow the caravan. The large bench seat meant that there was enough room for all five of us to sit up in the cab, which was handy. As usual, we planned to take our time over the trip, aiming to drive about two hundred miles each day and to stop off for the odd day here and there along the route.

From Adelaide, we set off east through Murray Bridge and across the wheat and sheep country of the Murray River Basin towards Pinnaroo and Ouyen. Here, out in the bush, the temperature started to soar and as we left Mildura and headed across the Hay Plains to Narrandera it became stinking hot, the sun beating down on a road that seemed to stretch straight ahead forever through about two hundred miles of the baking flatlands.

Then, suddenly, the weather changed. The wet season arrived early that year and by the time we reached Narrandera it was sheeting down and the Murray River was well in flood. We arrived at the caravan park to find that the water level had risen to the top of the banks and further upstream it had already overflowed and spread into the surrounding farmland so that it was a mile wide in some places, with many roads completely cut off.

Located between the Murray River on one side and a local creek on the other, the caravan park was soon ankle-deep in floodwater and we found ourselves marooned there for two or three days until it started to subside. This wasn't much fun for Vera and me, but, of course, the kids loved every minute of it, splashing around barefoot in the biggest puddles they had ever seen. As far as I was concerned, the only upside to it all was the plentiful supply of freshwater crayfish that we suddenly found wandering about the park. We were told that they didn't like the muddy water in the river and came out to seek the clearer water beyond the banks. They made very good eating and also very good fishing bait.

The truck didn't like the conditions at all. Every time we went through a patch of floodwater, the distributor got damp and we had to stop and dry the engine out. This was a continual problem until we got past the Lachlan River and up to Dubbo. Even spraying the electrics with a waterproof sealant didn't seem to help much.

We stayed in Dubbo for a couple of days, taking the opportunity to have a good clean-out in the caravan and to get the furniture in the back of the truck dried out. Even though the tarpaulin had protected it from the worst of the rain, the spray from the road had got everywhere, making everything damp.

While we were there we also found time to have a good look round this flourishing outback town, famous for its Western Plains Zoo and its old gaol, now a tourist attraction that includes the actual open-air gallows from which Jacky Underwood, one of the last of Australia's legendary 19th-century outlaws, or 'bushrangers', was hanged in 1901.

From Dubbo we pushed on up through New South Wales towards Moree and the Queensland border. With the temperature again up in the nineties, it was a wonderful relief to find, when we eventually arrived in Moree in the late afternoon, that the caravan park was right next door to the swimming pool. We wasted no time in setting up camp as quickly as possible and then dived in for a cooling swim and a paddle with the kids.

We were up and on our way again early the next morning and were only about eight miles north of Moree when we found a nice parking spot on the banks of the Gwydw River and decided to stop for some breakfast. After an hour or so we carried on, but the truck kept over-heating, which meant that we had to make regular stops. After lunch at Croppa Creek, we decided that we would go on along the Newell Highway as far as Bogabilla, thirty miles further on, and then call it a day and find somewhere to camp for the night.

It was now so hot that Vera decided to travel in the caravan with Lou and Kerri. It was a bit cooler there and she thought that maybe the girls would be able to get a bit of sleep. Tiff, meanwhile, stayed up front with me in the truck, lying comfortably on the seat. As I eased out onto the deserted highway I was in a happy and relaxed frame of mind, blissfully unaware of the bombshell that Fate was already aiming in my direction.

We had only gone about a mile or two like this when suddenly, quite out of the blue, there was the most almighty crash from behind and we were sent flying up the road. I first shot backwards in my seat before being hurled violently forwards against the steering wheel. At the same time, the back of the cab was forced forward so that I was trapped between the seat and the steering wheel. I looked round to see, thankfully, that Tiff had somehow stayed safely on the seat.

Frantic with worry and still not sure what was going on, it took me a few minutes to free myself but when I finally stumbled out onto the road the scene that greeted me was one of the most utter and terrible devastation. One horrified glance was enough to tell me what must have happened. We had been rammed from behind by a speeding 'semi', the name given to the vast articulated lorries that thunder to and fro across Australia. Much bigger than the juggernauts you get in the UK, these monster trucks also pull a second trailer.

A two-tier cattle truck, this particular one had veered off the road after hitting us, ploughing into the bush and flattening small trees before finally coming to rest about two hundred-and-fifty yards away. As for our caravan, there was simply nothing left of it. It had been completely demolished by the force of the impact, as had the back half of the truck. I knew instantly that nobody inside could pos-sibly have survived.

In a state of total shock, shaking from head to foot and with a sick feeling rising from the pit of my stomach, I staggered blindly along the roadside, hardly daring to look amongst the scattered bits of splintered wreckage for what I knew I would find there somewhere. There is no way to describe the overwhelming horror I felt as, one by one, I came across all three bodies – Vera, Lou and little Kerri. There was absolutely nothing that could be done for them. They must have died instantly. Blinded by tears and hardly knowing where I was or what I was doing, I searched around our scattered belongings and managed to find some blankets with which to cover them.

It was only then that I became aware of the truck driver standing nearby, unhurt but also, I imagine, in a state of shock. My grief and despair was suddenly replaced by blind rage. I had the .303 rifle that Norm had sold me in the cab of the truck and if I could have found the ammunition with which to load it, I swear I would have shot the driver there and then. As it was, I physically attacked him with my bare hands, kicking and punching. He was only saved from a severe beating thanks to the driver of a truck that had been following behind, who intervened to pull me off him.

Shocked and confused as I was, I could imagine just what must have caused the accident and my suspicions were to be borne out by the police investigations that followed. These big trucks had hand throttles to avoid the discomfort of having to keep your foot pressed non-stop on the accelerator for mile after mile on the long, straight Australian highways and you would often see drivers bowling along with their feet up on the dashboard and their hands resting on the steering wheel, while country music blasted out of the stereo. Some even had televisions in their cabs.

On blistering hot days, with the monotony of open and relatively deserted roads stretching straight ahead almost as far as the eye could see, it was all too easy to become drowsy and nod off. That is exactly what had happened in this case. It was only the impact of running into the back of the caravan that had startled the driver back to full consciousness, at which point he wrenched the wheel round and went ploughing across the bush. He must have been going at a tremendous lick as he came up behind us. Before filtering back onto the road to resume our journey after our lunch break in the lay-by at

Croppa Creek, I had obviously checked to see if anything was coming and, with clear visibility for some distance in either direction, there had been nothing in sight. And yet, less than two miles up the road he was on us.

The next few hours, days and weeks became a blur during which I was barely aware of what was going on around me and it was only much later that I was fully able to appreciate the kindness of the many people in the area who rallied round to help me and Tiff at this terrible time.

Among the first to arrive on the scene of the accident were Bill and Evol Sinclair. They lived on a farm just a mile away at Tooloona and were driving home from a shopping trip to Boggabilla when they found us. They were fantastic and immediately took charge of the whole, grim situation.

Having first done their best to calm me down a bit, they drove me and Tiff to Moree, where we were checked over by a doctor and where, still in a daze, I had to make statements to the police. When Bill and Evol then realised that we had no home to go to and nobody else we could turn to, they immediately insisted on taking us back to their place, with an invitation to stay there just as long as we wanted. In that way, they were true Good Samaritans, offering without hesitation to take us in despite the fact that we were complete strangers. As things turned out, we were to be with them for many weeks.

As news of the accident quickly spread, the entire local community started rallying round. Bill Price, the Sinclairs' nearest neighbour, even got together with the Mayor of Moree to start an appeal on our behalf that raised hundreds of dollars to help pay for the funerals.

These took place a week later at the Roman Catholic church in Toowoomba on what was, of course, an unbearably emotional and traumatic day for me. I don't remember too much about it because the doctor had put me on a heavy dose of valium, which pretty much knocked me out. However, one thing that still stands out in my memory to this day was the beautiful singing of the church choir, which, even in such awful circumstances, I found uplifting in some small way. The church was packed with people from the local community, most of whom I didn't know but who had heard or read about the accident and came to give moral support.

Among the friends who were present, Ron, my colleague on the meat inspection course, drove all the way from Adelaide with his wife just to be there. Like Bill and Evol, Ron was a pillar of strength throughout, although there was really nothing any of them could do to console me.

I was a broken man, totally shattered by the tragedy. For me, it was impossible to come to terms with the fact that almost my entire family had been wiped out in an instant, along with all our plans and hopes and dreams for the future. I was tormented by thoughts of how it might all have been avoided. If only we had not stopped for lunch at that particular spot, if only we had left five minutes later, if only we had all stayed in the truck … if only one could wind the clock back and do something just a little differently.

I found it difficult to accept that we had simply been in the wrong place at the wrong moment, and that this could have had such devastating repercussions, ending three innocent lives and tearing at least one other apart in the blink of an eye. The most terrible images kept flooding back into my mind. The only consolation was that Tiff had survived unscathed and was too young to have understood fully what had happened, or to have been too badly scarred psychologically.

Had it not been for her, I'm not sure that I would ever have learned how to cope or whether I could ever have got back on my feet after such a devastating blow. As it was, she gave me the will to live and as the weeks went by and the searing pain of my raw grief gave way to a dull, continuous ache, I gradually came to realise that I owed it to her to somehow pull myself together, to find the strength and the will to salvage something from the wreckage of my life.

CHAPTER 7

Filling The Void

Apart from little Tiffany, the accident had left me with absolutely nothing – no home, no job, no belongings, no money and, as far as I could bring myself to think about it in the immediate aftermath, not much of a future.

Our only home – the caravan – had been totally destroyed, along with all our possessions. Tiff and I had lost just about everything except the clothes we stood up in. At the same time, the bank account that I had held jointly with Vera had been frozen down in South Australia, pending valuation for death duties, which meant that I had no access to ready money. For the first few weeks afterwards I was completely dependant on Bill and Evol Sinclair in almost every way.

The accident happened on December 1st, 1973, and my recollections of the period leading up to Christmas are very hazy. Sedated with valium at first, I soon found that alcohol was an even more effective anaesthetic for the anguish I was suffering, helping to blot out the painful thoughts that otherwise filled my mind every hour of the day, and I regularly accompanied Bill to Moree or Goondiwindi to spend the evenings drinking in local bars, deliberately seeking oblivion. For a month, I was completely out of it.

As the New Year dawned, I realised that, if only for Tiff's sake, I had to try and haul myself out of the abyss and get some sort of normality back into both our lives, although at this stage I still wasn't able to think much beyond simple survival. I eventually managed to get a tractor-driving job on a neighbouring farm, ploughing and cultivating ready for the autumn sowing of wheat, sunflowers and sorghum. I would often be working all through the night, between sixteen and eighteen hours at a stretch, the mind-numbing monotony of it suiting my mood of deep despair. While all this was going on, Tiff was being looked after by Evol, who took her along on the school bus run that she drove each morning and evening. Evol also took her shopping to buy new clothes to replace those lost in the accident.

Bill's dad, Jim Sinclair, then took me on to work as a roustabout with his contract sheep shearing gang. This was another new experience for me. A roustabout is basically an odd-job man, responsible in this instance for penning the sheep, picking up the wool and generally cleaning up after the shearers. They were a bunch of tough and fairly colourful characters, who worked at an incredible speed, manhandling the sheep with practised ease. With the temperature in the shearing sheds well over 100°F, it was the hottest, sweatiest job I'd ever done and by the end of the day everybody would have worked up quite a thirst. We would often have to travel twenty or thirty miles to a job and the first stop on the way home would be at the nearest store, where a plentiful supply of 'coldies' would be purchased. I soon found that sitting in the sun in the back of the pick-up, knocking back the beers as we were driven along, was a quick way of getting tiddley and keeping at bay the depression that was never far away.

Meanwhile, Bill and I were spending even more time in the pubs as it became clear that his marriage to Evol was running into difficulties. He now needed to drown his sorrows almost as much as I did and I would often have to drive him home, much the worse for wear. He would collapse on the back seat of the old second hand car I had managed to buy by this time and, because he was six-foot-six-inches tall, he would have to lie with his feet sticking out of the window. I had to remember to make sure they were sticking out of the passenger side, not the driver's side, or a passing vehicle might have taken him off at the knee!

As his relationship with Evol became more and more strained, Bill moved out and into the shearers' quarters over at his parents' place. At the same time, Evol lined herself up with a job at a school more than one hundred and fifty miles away, down on the coast at Coffs Harbour. By now, the two of them were not even on speaking terms, so Bill asked me to drive her down there for the interview, unable to face the idea of driving three hundred miles there and back in silence. Having clinched the job, Evol then moved down to Coffs Harbour permanently. At the same time, Tiff and I left Tooloona and went to Moree, where we were invited to stay with Evol's sister, June, and her husband, Tommy.

I realised that before long I would have to find a place of my own, but with most of my money still tied up down in South Australia I was in a difficult situation. This problem was then solved when I went to look at caravans at a local dealership. On hearing my story, the owner, Ron Goodman, very kindly took me to his bank and helped me to arrange a loan so that I could buy a small second-hand caravan. Tommy and June then let me park it in their back yard and June looked after Tiff for me during the day while I went out to look for a new job, the seasonal ploughing and shearing work back at Tooloona having come to an end.

Tommy worked for the local Department of Main Roads and managed to set up a job interview for me there, as a result of which I was taken on to work with the bridge gang. This involved repairing and maintaining all the wooden bridges that crossed the rivers and creeks around Moree, some of them right out in the bush, as far as seventy miles away.

There were about half-a-dozen of us in the gang – truck driver Paddy Brennan, Richard Rush, Pete Duncan and a couple of Aborigines, Davo and Billo. Davo was a really nice guy and taught me a lot about bushcraft over the twelve months that I was with the DMR. Billo was a bit older and although he was very good to work with, he had had the odd spot of bother with the law from time to time, usually after having a bit too much to drink. I got on well with all of them and, although it took many months, I gradually found myself getting back to some sort of normality.

Apart from the fact that they were a good bunch of lads, I also enjoyed the job and that helped to take my mind off things. A lot of my time was spent on a swinging scaffold suspended under the bridge. I had no fear of heights, so I was quite happy up there and I was usually joined by Paddy Brennan. The mad one in the gang, he was the sort of character who wasn't bothered by anything. These days, Health & Safety would have a fit if they saw the makeshift scaffold, which we rigged up with ropes and a few planks, but one of the great advantages of working suspended under the bridge was that you were in the shade most of the day while, up above, the others were baking in the full sun.

We often found ourselves working on the large, twin-span Boolooroo Bridge. Located just north of Moree, this crossed over the Gwydir River, about thirty feet above the water. Sometimes, when it got really hot, we'd drop a couple of scaffolding planks into the water and have a race down the river, paddling the planks like canoes and then getting one of the gang to come and pick us up. The foreman knew exactly what we were up to, but was happy to turn a blind eye. As long as we got the work done on time, he didn't mind.

We would also take the opportunity to do a little fishing. We would simply set a few lines when we arrived in the morning and you could pretty much guarantee that by the time we left in the evening we would have caught two or three catfish, which we would sell to the lads back at the yard for a dollar a time, splitting the money between us. Our best customer was the general maintenance foreman, Eric Johnson, who was usually good for at least three or four fish every week. This was quite a nice little earner.

I did well in the job and was soon promoted to be bridge 'ganger', in charge of the team. My wages went up quite a bit with the extra responsibility, which was very useful. And, of course, with me in charge, the fishing and the racing continued unabated.

At around the same time, a new Chief Engineer took over at the depot. We called him Spook, because he was always sneaking up on us, trying to catch us out doing something wrong. He also had the annoying habit of standing on the riverbank below, bellowing orders at us and telling us how to do our job. This lasted until one day when he made the big mistake of coming up onto the scaffold with Paddy and me. Paddy waited until we were right above the middle of the river and then started jumping up and down, making the scaffold wobble and sway alarmingly. I've never seen anyone turn quite as white or hang on quite so tight as Spook did at that moment. We were always complaining about not having enough scaffolding boards, but after that incident we soon had what we wanted. And we no longer saw quite so much of Spook.

It was while I was with the DMR that the metric system was introduced in Australia. From then on, of course, everything had to be in kilometres instead of miles and one of our jobs was to paint out all the old milestones west of Moree. After about thirty miles, we were just beginning to get bored when we spotted a brood of emu chicks. Emu-chasing was a popular outback sport at the time, the idea being to try and grab a chick and race back to the safety of your vehicle with it before the mother bird could get you. This was quite a dangerous pastime because a full-grown emu is very quick and has one helluva kick. Of course, we'd always let the chicks go afterwards.

While we were out west I met and became friendly with Geoff and Tony, two other DMR boys who were working there. Meanwhile, Tommy had decided to leave the DMR and go back to farming. As his plans involved moving out of the house in Moree, it meant that I would have to look around for somewhere else to park my caravan. When I mentioned this to Tony he immediately said that I was welcome to move into his yard. This was a perfect arrangement as far as I was concerned since Tony and his wife, Val, had four kids and Val was only too happy to look after Tiff as well.

Tiff was now three-and-a-half years old. Although much too young to understand much about the accident, there had been heart-breaking moments in the days immediately afterwards when she would keep asking where her mummy was and where Lou and Kerri had gone. And when I started going out to work again she would scream in panic as soon as I tried to leave the house, so that I would have to slip out quietly, without her noticing, while Val distracted her attention. But gradually she seemed to adjust to the new situation and with Tony and Val's children for company she seemed much happier.

As for me, it was many months before the raw grief started to heal and even then there was never an hour that went by when I didn't find my thoughts turning to Vera and my two little girls. Their loss had left a gaping void in my life that I knew could not be filled and I was resigned to the sad fact that things would never be quite the same again. At the same time, I gradually came to realise that I had to get on with my life despite the emptiness I felt.

My social life at this time was restricted to the odd night out with Tony and Geoff at the local R.S.L Club, the equivalent of the British Legion, where we would go to have a few beers and play the one-armed bandits. It never occurred to me that I would ever find anyone to replace Vera – and I probably wouldn't have done if it hadn't been for Tiff. Nearly a year had passed since the accident when I happened to be introduced to Geoff's former sister-in-law, Fay, a divorcee with a daughter, Penny, who was a little bit older than Tiff. The two girls got on well and Fay kindly agreed to look after Tiff while I was out at work, which was obviously an ideal arrangement. Both being on our own for different reasons, she and I then gradually drifted together and, after a while, she and Penny moved in with Tiff and me.

Meanwhile, with the bridge job coming to an end thanks to a re-organisation within the DMR, I put in for a transfer to the same road gang that Geoff was working with. A new highway was being built about forty-five miles west of Moree and for a short while we were transported out there on a daily basis. However, although we got paid an extra travel allowance this made for a very long day, so the DMR decided to build a camp on the site. We'd go out there on a Sunday night or first thing Monday morning, come home for the night on Wednesday, then go back on Thursday morning and home again on Friday night.

Out on the site we were living in Portakabins. Outside, the galley consisted of two long brick walls with a big sheet of steel over the top. With a large wood fire underneath, this served as a giant hotplate. To get the wood, we would take out one of the bulldozers, push over a few dead trees and then run over them to break them up into man-ageable logs. It was surprising how many snakes and lizards were hiding in these hollow trees. And as some of the snakes were highly poisonous, you had to be very careful.

My first job out on the site was to drive a heavy-duty roller. Boring in the extreme, this involved going endlessly backwards and forwards all day, compacting the gravel base after the graders had levelled it off. Geoff was the No 1 grader driver and he soon showed me how to operate one of these machines, which were a bit more interesting than the roller, and I was then sent further out west to work on dirt road maintenance.

One day when Geoff and I were working south of Moree, two big semi-trailers collided nearby on the Newell Highway, one of them full of sunflower oil and the other carrying a cargo of sweets and chocolates. We were sent along to clear up the mess and I can still picture Geoff with a big smile on his face, driving his grader along while stuffing After-Eight mints down his throat as fast as he could. The health authority having condemned the lot, we loaded up our truck with as much as we could collect and took it back to the depot where we shared it out among the rest of the lads. I also took a load home for Tiff and Penny, who ate so many sweets that they made themselves sick.

It was once again getting close to Christmas and with the girls due to start school in the New Year, Fay and I decided to move to a caravan park on the other side of town that was nearer to the school. The caravan I had at the time wasn't big enough for the four of us, so we went up to Warwick and bought a new, eight-berth, 26-footer. As my money was still tied up in South Australia, this again meant taking out a loan.

On the new site, we soon became friendly with the couple in the caravan next door. I knew the husband, Richard, having worked with him occasionally during my time on the bridge gang. It turned out he had a second job on a farm east of Moree known as Bundy Station and he managed to get me in there as well. With the loan for the new caravan to pay off, this was very handy.

Bundy Station covered about 7,500 acres and was owned by an American, Kenny Carpenter, and his son, Lee. Kenny fulfilled the role of the rancher, while Lee was more of a cowboy, looking after all the beef cattle. Richard and I, meanwhile, spent every weekend either ploughing and cultivating or working on land clearance, ripping out scrub to create more wheat fields.

Fay and I and the girls were invited to spend Christmas Day with Geoff and Shirley and their three kids. For anyone who has grown up in the UK, Christmas Down Under always seems a bit strange. For a start, of course, December 25th falls in early summer in Australia, so for those of us accustomed to dreaming of a traditional white Christmas with all the old familiar trimmings, it's not that easy to get into the right festive mood. For instance, you don't have much of an appetite for turkey and plum pudding when the sun's blazing down and you're sweltering in 80° or more! Instead, most people prefer to take a picnic down to the nearest beach.

In some ways, it was a relief not to have quite so much of the commercialism that has become such an unattractive feature of Christmas in this country, where the countdown to the big day seems to get longer and longer and the first tinselly television ads start appearing as early as October. Everything is a bit more laid back in Australia. They still have a Father Christmas in the big department stores – although he's usually got shorts on underneath his outfit! And although there was no chimney in the caravan for Santa to come down, we always made sure the kids had their stockings filled with presents.

After spending Christmas Day with Geoff and Shirley, we were then joined by Fay's parents, Ted and Edna, who came to spend a few days with us. They were living up in the Australian gemfields in a place called Sapphire, about five hundred miles north of Moree, where they had been running a sapphire mining business with two of their four sons. This sounded quite exciting and although Ted had just sold the business, he assured me that there was still plenty of money to be made out of sapphire mining if you were prepared to take a gamble and work like mad.

This idea immediately appealed to me, but with the new caravan still to be paid for and a bigger and better car now needed to pull it, I realised we would have to stay put for a while. I had to take out yet another loan to buy the V8 Ford Fairlaine I'd had my eye on, but by working all hours with the DMR during the week and at Bundy Station at weekends, I soon paid off both that and the loan for the caravan. Meanwhile, Tiff and Penny had both started school at the local nursery.

Throughout this time, I had been fighting through a solicitor for compensation for the accident from the owners of the semi-trailer, a firm of livestock transporters based in Dubbo. This process was to drag on for another eight years and involved me in repeated trips down to Sydney to be checked over by medical specialists. Later on, after Fay and I moved up to Sapphire to join her parents, this entailed a round trip of two thousand miles that took two days each time.

When, in 1983, the firm's insurers did eventually agree on a settlement, it was for just A$25,000, of which A$4,000 immediately went on legal fees. Given the circumstances, it didn't seem very much – not that anything could have made up for the loss I had suffered. As for the driver of the semi, he somehow managed to get away with a fine of A$175 and a three month ban after pleading guilty to the relatively minor charge of driving without due care and attention. Nobody could prove what we all suspected, which was that had been asleep at the wheel. I was left with a bitter sense of injustice.

It was over the Easter weekend of 1975 that Fay and I first visited her parents up in Sapphire. We set off on the 500-mile trip as soon as I finished work on the Thursday evening and drove through the night. With fuel running low, we eventually stopped off at Rolleston in the early hours of the morning and snatched a bit of sleep at the roadside while waiting for the petrol station to open. Arriving in Sapphire later that day, we found ourselves in what was very much a 'one-horse town'. Consisting of no more than a dozen fairly basic houses and a few others that were little more than tin sheds, plus a post office and the Blue Gem general store, it reminded me of one of those Wild West cowboy towns, except that it didn't even have a saloon!

Ted and Edna lived in a caravan on the site of one of the claims they had been working. The van had a tin awning extending from one side, with an outside toilet that was built over an old mine shaft they had dug out a few years earlier. It was all fairly basic. And with their two younger sons, John and Jeff, still living with them, it was also very cramped. Fay and I had to sleep under the tin awning while Tiff and Penny bedded down in the car. With no mozzie nets to protect us, Fay and I were kept awake most of the night and ended up smothered in bites.

Despite the discomfort, I thoroughly enjoyed the weekend, during which Ted gave me a guided tour of the area, filling me in on how everything worked and introducing me to some of the miners. A lot of what I saw and heard reminded me of the great American Gold Rush that I knew about from books and films and I found it all extremely interesting.

The first sapphires were found in central Queensland in about 1870 and when they then became fashionable among the aristocrats of Tsarist Russia, the price rocketed. More than a thousand prospectors descended on the remote area around Anakie, where the main settlements were named Sapphire, Emerald and Rubyvale. People were drawn by stories such as that of a legendary figure known only as 'Darky', who was said to have made a vast fortune simply by wheeling his barrow onto a field, staking his claim and almost immediately unearthing a huge concentration of gems just beneath the surface. Following the Russian Revolution and the consequent disappearance of the market for sapphires there, the industry then went into decline and fluctuated weakly for some years until the late 1950s and early 1960s when the arrival of buyers from overseas – in particular, from Thailand – sparked a fresh boom.

Up until that time, most of the mining had been done by hand and was very much like the most basic form of gold prospecting. Shallow 'paydirt', the strata in which the gems were concentrated, would be dug from a depth of no more than a few feet before being washed and sieved to separate out the various different coloured chips of the crystallized mineral known as corundum – mostly blue, green and yellow sapphires and some red rubies. When I first visited Sapphire there were still plenty of people working in this way, including quite a lot of true 'fossickers' – amateur prospectors, including a few tourists, who would often come up just for the weekend, scratching around in the hope of stumbling across another 'Golden Queen', 'Anderson's Yellow' or 'Black Star of Queensland', three of the largest stones ever found, each worth thousands of dollars. At the same time, machine mining was on the increase among full-time prospectors who, in order to make a decent living, needed to operate on a commercial scale, digging down thirty feet or more to the deeper seams of paydirt, known as 'washes', and processing it, tons at a time, through motor-driven washing plants.

All this rather appealed to my sense of adventure. However, conditions in Ted and Edna's caravan were very cramped and by the end of the weekend Fay and I were only too glad to get away and head back to civilisation and the comforts of home. However, we did agree to return later in the year to help Ted build the house that he planned to put up on a plot of land that he had bought with part of the proceeds from selling his mining business. Characteristically, he kept the money, in cash, in a tin box in the boot of his car. Like quite a few people living up in the gemfields, he didn't believe in banks.

Sapphire had a caravan park where we thought we might stay on our return. Although it did have shower and laundry facilities, it was still fairly basic – to get hot water for the shower, for example, you had to light a large wood fire under the boiler! But at least the set-up would be a bit more comfortable than it had been under Ted and Edna's awning.

After a few months back in Moree, I began to get restless again. Jobwise, there was nothing much doing at Bundy station once the ploughing had been done and the following year's crop sown, so the weekend work there gradually dried up. I still had my regular job with the DMR, working out west with the road gang and living in the barracks during the week, but as winter set in it began to get very cold in the cabins at night, another good reason to think about heading north to the warmer weather. As soon as the kids finished school in December, I quit the DMR and we packed everything up and set off back to Sapphire.

I'd never previously towed quite such a large caravan as the 26-footer and so, to be on the safe side, I fitted double sway bars along with electric brakes. We decided to follow a slightly different route this time, one that included a few long stretches of dirt road through some quite remote parts of the outback. This was partly for the kids' benefit, so that they could get to see a bit more of the country and its wildlife. Sure enough, we spotted plenty of kangaroos and wallabies along the way as well as wild horses and wild pigs.

We came across several litters of piglets at one point and with the girls both 'oohing' and 'aahing' over these cute little creatures I thought it best not to tell them too much about the pig-chasing which, along with emu-chasing, was a favourite off-duty pastime for me and the rest of the road gang when we were working out west in the bush. We'd go off in search of a litter of young ones, with the aim of catching a few and taking them home to be fattened up in a mate's sty. Once they were big enough, they would then be slaughtered and the meat shared out and stuck in the freezer. It made for very good eating, the flavour being much better than that of domestic pork.

The chase itself was also very good sport, although it could be even more dangerous than the previously mentioned pursuit of emu chicks if the parents were to catch up with you. A good kicking from an adult emu could be extremely unpleasant, but a wild pig had the potential to do much more serious damage, its lethal tusks all too easily capable of ripping you open. As soon as you managed to grab hold of a piglet it would start squealing, at which point you had to run like hell for the safety of the pick-up truck, with the enraged parents in hot pursuit. It was advisable to have a mate standing by with a rifle, just in case you weren't quick enough on your feet.

Having this time taken the scenic route on the way up from Moree, it was midnight before we reached Rolleston. With the caravan site closed, we again had to park in the main street for the night, filling up with fuel as soon as the garage opened the next morning and continuing our journey. Our next stop was at Emerald, where we stocked up with groceries, the prices out in the minefields being very high. From there it was about thirty miles to Sapphire, where we eventually arrived at around noon, having been on the road for about eighteen hours.

With only a couple of weeks to go before Christmas, we settled into the caravan park and set about trying to get our bearings. Penny and Tiff were enrolled at the local school in Anakie, about eight miles away. Very conveniently, there was a school bus that would pick them up right outside the park each morning and drop them back again in the afternoon.

Describing itself as 'the Gateway to the Gemfields', Anakie was actually smaller than Sapphire and not much more impressive, although as well as the school it did also boast a railway station (through which trains passed two or three times a week), a run-down motel, a pub into which you could just about get twenty people at a pinch, a post office and a small take-away that sold hamburgers and hot dogs.

Little did we ever imagine as we explored the area that this rather God-forsaken place in the back of beyond was to be our home for several years to come.

CHAPTER 8

Precious Stones

I got my first taste of prospecting very shortly after arriving in Sapphire.

The rainy season had just started when we got there and it was John, one of Ted and Edna's four sons, who introduced me to the art of 'specking'. This was the most basic form of 'fossicking' and involved waiting until just after there had been a real downpour before going out onto ground that had already been worked out and abandoned. Here, with a careful eye and a bit of luck, you could often pick up little bits of sapphire that had been washed off the old workings by the rain. Sometimes, you might even happen across quite a decent-sized stone that had been missed by the original miners. We did quite well and soon had enough of a 'parcel' of stones to sell to the Thai buyers for a few hundred dollars worth of pocket money.

This was yet another new adventure for me and seemed a bit like playing the 'pokies', the fruit machines that were such a fixture in every Aussie club and bar. As with the one-armed bandits, you never knew quite what was coming up next. In the same sort of way, it was also quite addictive.

Once Christmas was over, however, the building of Ted and Edna's house became the main priority. I'd never built a house from scratch before, so it was a case of having to learn as I went along. Ted and I first had to dig the footings out by hand before laying the concrete foundations, using a small mixer that we had managed to borrow from a mate of his down the road. Next, we had to build the walls up to floor level, with Ted mixing the mortar and carting the blocks and me laying them. All this was very hard work and seemed to take forever.

Putting the concrete floor down was a big job, but it was made easier by the fact that we had help from both John and his younger brother Jeff, plus the use of a second mixer. We got the whole floor done in a day – and celebrated with a carton of 'coldies'. After that, it was time for me to start building the walls. This was fairly straight-forward as it was only a single storey, two-bedroom house.

At the time, John was working for the machinery miner who had bought Ted's business and he was able to borrow a truck and a dumper to shift the blocks around and also to get sand and gravel out of the local creek. Once the walls were up and the roof was on, another of Ted's mates came along to do the wiring and put in all the electrics. All it needed then was for me to plaster the inside walls and do all the painting and it was ready for Ted and Edna to move in.

The whole job had taken just five weeks, and given that I'd had vir-tually no previous experience, I was rather proud of my handiwork. At the same time, I was just about worn out. However, there was no time to take it easy. Still owing money on the Fairlaine, I had to find a job, pronto. Fortunately, it turned out that Gordon Graham, John's boss, was looking for a truck driver to cart the paydirt from his various claims to the washing plants, where Ted also managed to get himself a job.

Although Ted had sold most of his business to Gordon, he had kept one un-worked claim down in what they called the Rush, and at weekends and on days off we started to sink a shaft. It was all pick and shovel work, but after a few days we eventually hit paydirt, fifteen feet down. By begging and scrounging bits and pieces, we rigged up a Willoughby and started our own small washing operation. This was the beginning of my serious mining activities.

Ted and I sorted all the stones that we found and put them in a jar, and by the time the paydirt ran out in that first shaft we had fifteen hundred dollars worth of sapphires to sell. Split between us, that gave me enough to pay off the car loan, while Ted had the cash needed to put the finishing touches to his house.

Encouraged by this success, we sank another shaft, but this wasn't nearly so productive. After working the whole of each weekend and at every other spare moment in between for a month, we ended up with just $500-worth of stones between us. Fortunately, we still had our jobs with Gordon, so this was just extra pocket money. The other advantage of working for Gordon was that I learned a lot about the mining business just by watching what was going on.

There were a few bits of spare ground just behind the caravan park, in between the old registered claims. The paydirt here was only just below the surface and I decided to do a little fossicking there one Saturday afternoon and soon came up with quite a few decent sapphires. I showed them to Ted, who got quite excited, and on the Sunday he and I went back together and spent all day digging there. By the end of the day, we had over two hundred dollars worth of stones. After very carefully covering up all signs of our activity, just to make sure that nobody else cottoned on to what we were doing, we returned again the following weekend in the hope of further success, but although we did find a few more stones, the ground ran out fairly quickly. And although we dug all around the surrounding area we never again found another pocket like that first one.

Having satisfied ourselves that there was nothing left there, we returned to Ted's claim and sank a third shaft. However, after a great deal more hard work all we had to show for our efforts was about three dollars worth of rubbish stone. With the ground getting deeper and the paydirt running out, we gave that up as a bad job.

Shortly after this, things got even more desperate when John and Ted fell out with Gordon and jacked in their jobs with him. As I was a mate of theirs, Gordon then started to make my life very difficult, so I, too, walked out. With nothing else to do, the three of us went back to the shallow ground and scratched a very meagre living there. At the same time, we'd sneak off and go specking on Gordon's ground every time it rained heavily, knowing that he wouldn't be around if the weather was bad. Whenever there was a real downpour and the machine mining had to stop, he would be off drinking in the pub or womanising in Emerald – so we knew we wouldn't be spotted.

However, it soon became clear that we weren't going to be able to survive on these slim pickings alone, so when people who had watched me putting up Ted's house started approaching me about doing the odd bit of building work for them, I jumped at the opportunity. The first couple of jobs involved putting in septic tanks and I then built a small house for the postmistress, based on the same single storey design as Ted's place. While I was working on this, one of the leading machinery miners from Rubyvale asked me to build a large extension for him. This was a big project that would entail several months' work, so I brought in Ted to give me a hand.

It was while we were working on this job that I had a couple of bits of really good luck. Firstly, the lease on a plot of land located on a bank above the caravan park came up for sale. It was owned by an old boy known as 'Dirty Percy', who lived in a filthy old caravan parked permanently on the site. He cooked all his meals on an open fire and his toilet consisted of a few sheets of corrugated iron roughly nailed to a couple of nearby trees, with a plank of wood to sit on. Although his so-called homestead lease gave him the legal right to put up a house on the land, he was too old to build it himself and, anyway, his daughter wanted to move him into an old folks' home in Emerald, where he could be properly looked after. As soon as I heard about this, I went up to see Percy and managed to buy the plot off him for two hundred dollars.

Ray, the mining boss for whom I was building the extension, kindly agreed to let me use his bulldozer to level the site and to create a dam in which to collect rainwater. The second bit of luck then came when Ray also tipped me off that he had heard on the grapevine that certain areas of Crown Land in the mining fields were to be opened up and that this would allow Ted and I each to peg two five-acre leases for machinery mining.

We straightaway drove into town to purchase a chainsaw and spent all the next day cutting posts, ready to mark out our claims. We needed five sturdy six-foot posts per claim, one for each corner plus an extra 'surveying' post to which would be attached a notice giving details of the claim – the time and date when it was pegged and the name of the claimant. When the official announcement was made a couple of days later that the land was up for grabs all hell broke loose, with people racing around trying to peg as much of the most promising ground as they could. We, of course, had the considerable advantage of a head start.

The scene there really was exactly like something out of the Gold Rush days in the Wild West. There were no gun laws in force in Australia at the time and, like everybody else, we always carried a rifle, just in case someone tried to steal our ground. We heard later that one chap had actually been shot in the arm during an argument over a disputed claim, although this incident took place a mile or two away from where we were.

Ted and I pegged our own claims, plus a couple each for both Edna and Fay. It was then a case of getting them properly surveyed and registered with the Mines Department at Clermont. Once that had been done, we had to wait for the claims to be inspected and the formalities completed before the licenses could be granted, a process that would take several weeks.

In the meantime, having finished Ray's extension, I decided to start work on my own house. However, with money running low again I also needed to find another paid job to keep me going. It was then that Willy Litz, the German-born owner of the caravan park, came up trumps. Willy, another machinery miner, had just built a new washing plant and needed a night shift driver for the loader, which fed the paydirt into the plant. The hours were long and hard, from six at night until six the next morning, but this suited me perfectly, since it gave me the time to work on the house during the day.

Over the next five weeks, I got the foundations in, the floor down, the walls up and most of the corrugated iron roof on, at which point Fay and I decided to sell the caravan and move in. We bought a couple of new beds for Penny and Tiff, while we ourselves slept on a mattress on the floor in the living room until I was able to raise enough money to finish off the last bit of the roof above our bedroom. With drinking water from the rainwater tank that I had installed and water for the shower and toilet coming from the dam, we had everything we needed.

Meanwhile, I had my first experience of claim jumping when a couple of miners, one armed with a camera, tried to peg some of Willy Litz's land. As soon as Willy got wind of this, a bunch of us – including one of Willy's men who claimed to be a former Swedish boxing champion – went up to sort it out. While the foreman grabbed the camera off one of the interlopers, I got hold of the other and rubbed his nose in the dirt. We were fully intending to chuck him in the slurry dam, but he managed to break loose and hightailed it out of the place in his pick-up. Not long after this, Ted and I had a similar spot of bother with a bloke who tried to overpeg one of our claims, but he soon thought better of the idea and backed off when I threatened him with a brickie's trowel!

As soon as our licences finally came through we hired a digger and dug a test hole on the lowest part of what we thought was probably the best of our claims. We soon hit a 'wash', a sapphire-bearing seam that, in this case, turned out to be about five foot wide and extended down about sixteen foot to the 'floor'. After hand-washing a few bucketfuls, the paydirt looked very promising, so we wasted no time in hiring our mate Eddie to put in a proper 'cut' with his bulldozer. We then washed a sample through his plant and were more than pleasantly surprised when this indicated a healthy average yield of A$6 worth of sapphires to the yard. We were in business!

The first thing we needed to do was to set up our own washing plant. With this in mind, we bought an old disused claim nearby that had a large waterhole on it. We then managed to get hold of a second-hand bin, for hosing in the dirt, and a pulsator to do the actual washing. We also rigged up a screen for separating the sand and the larger rocks out of the wash – which, in its raw state, looks a bit like river gravel. And we put together a makeshift loader that we called 'the flying teaspoon' and which featured a two-wheel drive, a small bucket and a crash gearbox. The only new item we had to buy was a Honda water pump.

Within a few days we had the whole system up and running. I screened the excavated dirt and drove the loader, while Ted hosed in the dirt and looked after the washing plant. It was only a very small set-up, but by working flat out from about 8am to 6pm, we were soon managing to process about one hundred yards of paydirt a day.

Our first setback came after eight days when the motor on the loader blew up, bringing us to a complete standstill. Happily, after a few frantic phone calls, we succeeded in acquiring the spare parts needed to fix the problem and soon got it going again. Meanwhile,

Fay and Edna were busy sorting the stones by size (firsts, seconds and thirds) and quality (colours, specials, fines and industrial corundum) and preparing our first big 'parcel' for the Thai buyers, who made regular visits to the gemfields. By the time we were ready to go in and see them in Rubyvale, we had collected nearly fifty ounces and, after a lot of bargaining, a price of A$80-a-ounce was agreed, working out at a total of around A$4,000. Even after paying for the hire of the bulldozer and the repairs to the loader, this still left us with a very handsome profit.

By the time we had finished washing the rest of the dirt from that first cut, we had enough for another, similar parcel. This enabled me to put all the finishing touches to my house. Painted white outside, it soon became known locally as The White House and was the envy of everybody, one of the best homes to be found anywhere in the mining fields.

Already flushed with success, Ted and I now put in a second cut and this proved to be even better and more lucrative than the first. It also had the added advantage of being only twelve feet deep, which meant that we didn't have to pay quite so much to hire the bulldozer, which could be an expensive business. However, we did have a few problems with the water pump, which wasn't really big enough for the job, and decided we would have to invest in a brand new Lister diesel. Even so, we were well ahead financially by the time we finished washing the second cut and it seemed there would be no looking back.

After taking the kids for a short holiday over on the coast, we decided to put in a big, six-blade cut – as against the two-blade cuts we had been doing up until then – the idea being to get a really good supply of dirt out before the rainy season set in and hampered operations on the wet ground. As a result, we were left with a small mountain of six thousand yards of dirt to process. However, our luck, it now seemed, was changing. As we got stuck into the screening and washing, often working twelve-hour days, the yield gradually went down from six dollars-a-yard to four dollars and then to three. By the time we had got through the whole six thousand yards we were feeling pretty despondent.

To make matters worse, Ted was starting to suffer with a very bad back. This was the legacy of an accident he'd had years before when he was working as a sheep shearer and a heavy wool press had fallen on him. As far as he was concerned, the disappointment of the large cut, coming on top of the physical strain and the chronic pain it was causing him, proved the final straw and he decided that he wanted to sell his half share of the business and asked me if I would buy him out. I invited him to name his price, and after a bit of thought, he reckoned that the land and the business together must be worth sixty thousand dollars.

This frightened the living daylights out of me at first, but being a bit of a gambler, I went to see the bank manager about a loan. With the money I already had in the bank, I needed to borrow A$10,000 in order to give Ted a down payment of fifteen thousand dollars, with the second fifteen thousand to follow six months later. Having successfully negotiated this loan, I then went straight out and put myself even deeper in hock by buying the claim next door for A$3,000. The miner I bought it from had been working the side furthest away from us without any success, but the nearside bordered the area where we had made our very lucrative second cut, so I reckoned there was a good chance I might strike lucky again.

Once I'd done the deal with Ted I wasted no time before putting in the first cut on the ground I'd just bought and it looked promising straightaway. Jeff, Ted's youngest son, had finished school by this time, so I hired him to take his dad's place on the washing plant and we set to work on the pile of paydirt. We washed it all in eleven days and I ended up with a parcel of stone worth A$13,000. Bingo!

With money like this coming in, it was time consider buying a better loader to replace the old flying teaspoon. I flew down to Brisbane with Fay and the kids and after first enjoying a couple of days holiday, purchased a second-hand Hough 30, a superior four-wheel drive machine. This was four times the size of the teaspoon and much easier to operate, meaning that I would be able to speed up the whole screening and washing process. Within three or four months, I had paid off all my debts and was well ahead.

With the kids away at school all day, Fay was now doing all the sorting of the stones and we were getting bigger and better parcels to sell. We were also starting to keep quite a few stones to have cut for ourselves, a job that was done by our next-door neighbour, Bob. A full-time gem cutter, Bob lived with his wife and two daughters in a pair of Portakabins and was one of the more respectable members of the local mining community.

Not surprisingly, a lot of the characters you came across in the gemfields were real rough diamonds. However, despite appearances they often had hearts of gold underneath it all. Fairly typical was a chap called Keith Smith, known to one and all as 'Big Smithy' on account of being over six feet tall and about eighteen stone in weight. A contract bulldozer driver by trade, he had an appetite for both food and booze to match his size.

We sometimes used to go round to his place for barbecues and it wasn't unusual to see him eat half-a-dozen steaks at a sitting. His favourite tipple was a brand of cheap white wine that came in little stubby bottles and he would always start by opening two of these and swigging them both down in one go, together! He'd then have another 'double' before slowing down to just one at a time. He could quite easily get through a dozen of these bottles in the first couple of hours after he finished work, without apparently being any the worse for wear.

Immensely strong, he would occasionally have to replace the cutting edge of the dozer blade and when he tightened the bolts he would do them up with such force that not even two men together could undo them. Despite this, he was a gentle giant of a man – although, like many people you met out on the mining fields, he'd had his fair share of trouble with the authorities in the past. He told me that before coming up to Sapphire he had been sand quarrying down in Southern Queensland, where he was operating six bulldozers. At some point the taxman had come after him and, knowing that all his dozers were likely to be confiscated in lieu of the tax he owed, he buried two of them in the sand so that they wouldn't be found. He then dug them up later and brought them up to the gemfields to get started again there.

Working for Big Smithy was another dozer driver known as

Scottish Jock. Again, he was a big lad who looked like the sort of bloke you would do well to keep on the right side of. In this respect, his reputation was sealed by one legendary incident. Up where we were, law enforcement was virtually non-existent. There were a couple of part-time coppers seven or eight miles away in Anakie, but they were rarely seen in our neck of the woods – until, that is, the arrival on the scene of a keen new recruit who quickly acquired the nickname 'Super Trooper'. He decided he was going to tame the mining fields, getting everybody to register their vehicles – something that most of them never bothered to do – and generally introducing the letter of the law.

This caused considerable resentment and it wasn't long before a couple of drunk miners set upon him one night and were in the process of beating the living daylights out of him when Scottish Jock stepped in to save him from almost certain death. We didn't see much of Super Trooper after that – and everybody made sure they behaved themselves when Scottish Jock was around!

And then there was prospector Fred Walker. He was even bigger than Big Smithy and Scottish Jock. He must have weighed twenty stone and was as strong as an ox, capable of digging a trench, twenty foot deep, in a day – by hand! I met him on my first visit to Sapphire, when Ted took me out to show me around the area. A true eccentric, with a great bushy beard, he lived way out in the bush, five or six miles from anywhere, his home being a tin hut that was just about big enough for a bed and not much else. Outside was a very basic dunny, while all his cooking was done on a makeshift barbecue. When Ted took me to see him early one morning, he emerged from his hut looking rather bleary-eyed, his beard covered in feathers. It was an alarming sight.

"Strewth! Whatever happened to you, Fred?" cried Ted.

"Oh, I had a fight last night," drawled Fred in reply, scratching his head and adding after a pause: "With me pillow!"

Fred was famous for having mined one of the biggest green sapphires ever found. But although he was offered huge amounts of money for it – it was reckoned to be worth between A$20,000 and A$30,000 – he refused to sell. What's more, he kept it in an old ammunition box under the seat of his ancient Land Rover, along with all his other stones. Like Ted, he didn't believe in banks. Anyway, this stone was stolen about three times, but because everybody knew where it came from, the thieves could never sell it on and, somehow or other, it always ended up back with Fred.

Of all the many strange and eccentric characters we came across up there, the most unlikely were 'Hippie' Bruce and his wife Martha. They had the claim next to one of mine and, like Fred Walker, they lived in a tin hut on the site. Total hippies, they did a bit of hand mining but didn't seem that serious about it. They were much more interested in growing their own marijuana out in the bush. And when they got on the pot, they and their friends would run around stark naked, jumping in and out of the dam where they stored the water for their shower.

They were nice guys, completely harmless and, in traditional hippie fashion, very laid back in every way. Bruce even invited me to machine mine on his ground if I wanted to. "Hey, man, help yourself," he told me airily, taking another puff on an enormous spliff. "There's no way I can get at it myself, just by hand, so you're welcome to have a go." He was equally generous when I ran into a slight technical problem on my claim.

With everything going so well, I had decided it was time to upgrade the washing plant again. I first got a local engineer to build me a new piano wire shaker, the strands of piano wire being much more efficient that the usual mesh, which all too easily got clogged up. This worked well for a time, but with all the dust flying around, the petrol engine soon started seizing up. I wanted to replace it with an electric motor, but the problem here was that I didn't have electricity down on the claim. Bruce, however, was actually connected to the mains (one of his few concessions to conventional living) and he immediately agreed to a deal whereby I offered to pay his entire electricity bill if he would let me plug into his supply.

Next, I decided I needed to get myself a small truck. We were working further and further away from the washing plant, too far to cart the dirt in the loader, one bucket at a time. So, it was off to Brisbane again to search for a suitable vehicle. We decided to make it a family trip, with Ted and Jeff driving everybody down in two cars, leaving me free to come back in whatever truck I managed to buy. After combing the city I found a little D500 tipper that was perfect for the job.

We had hardly started on the 500-mile trip back when the brakes on the truck started to stick. Luckily, I'd brought my toolbox with me and after a bit of cursing and swearing I managed to make the necessary running repairs. By now, it was pouring with rain and it continued like that for the rest of the day, making driving conditions very difficult. We struggled on as far as Moura, but by then it was pitch dark and with a forty-mile section of dirt road ahead of us, which could be dodgy at the best of times, we opted to stop off in a motel for the night.

The next morning we got up to find that although the rain had stopped, the road was waterlogged and completely flooded in places. It was a case of fuelling up and then, once we got onto the dirt road section, going like hell and not stopping for anything, in case we got stuck. I went first, in the truck, with Ted and Jeff following in the two cars and when I got back onto the tarmac at the other end I had to wait half-an-hour for the others to arrive. Their cars were covered in black mud, Ted complaining bitterly that there had been moments when he didn't think he was going to make it. Once I'd got over this exhausting trip, it was back to work with a vengeance to make up for lost time.

Not that it was all work and no play during this time. Together with Ted and his two boys, John and Jeff, I managed to do quite a bit of fishing in the local rivers and creeks. Ted was an old bushman from way back and he taught me a great deal about fishing the big rivers out west. He sometimes used what he called his 'square hook' – a net strung across the river. This was perfectly legal, as long as the net conformed to certain size regulations, and we caught no end of fish that way.

Our expeditions mostly took place in the cooler months, when there was no risk of the sudden floods that you got in the wet season. Sometimes, we'd camp out all night on the riverbank, cooking some of the fish we caught over the campfire for tea and breakfast. We'd take plenty of block ice in a large cooler box filled with cold beers. When we'd drunk them, there'd be room in the cooler box for the rest of the catch that we were taking home.

A favourite place for a night's fishing was Selma Weir, out near Emerald. We'd sometimes take the kids along with us when we went there. We'd set our lines and then sit around the campfire, enjoying a few beers and feeding bread and cold chicken to the possums that came down out of the trees. The kids loved that.

The mozzies were always a bit of a problem on the riverbank, but the anti-mozzie spray, along with the smoke from the fire, helped to keep them at bay. If the spray ran out, the best thing to do was to burn dry cow dung on the fire – another tip I learned from Ted.

On one occasion Ted caught a large sleepy cod that must have weighed about six pounds. After scaling and cleaning it and sprinkling it with salt and pepper, he wrapped it in a soaking wet brown paper bag and placed it among the warm ashes on the edge of the campfire. He waited until the paper was completely dry and had just started to catch light before pulling it out of the ashes. He then peeled the paper off and there inside, perfectly cooked, was the most delicious fish I have ever tasted.

Apart from fishing and drinking, there wasn't an awful lot to do up in the gemfields. There was a drive-in cinema thirty miles away from us in Emerald and we also used to go water-skiing near there on Fairbairn Dam. A mate of mine called Russell Doughty had a powerboat with a big V8 in-board engine and he taught me how to ski barefoot. With his big size 12 feet, he was quite an expert.

In Sapphire, the highlights of the social calendar were the twice-yearly horse race meetings at the local bush racecourse. This was just across the road from our house. The course only had an inside rail and the whole set-up was generally pretty basic, but people came from miles around and the bookies did a roaring trade.

By the end of 1977 the mining business was going so well that I felt able to trade in the Fairlaine for a brand new soft-top Suzuki that I'd had my eye on for some time – the first new car I'd ever owned. It was bright red, and coming up to Christmas that year we decided to turn it into Santa's sleigh and give all the local kids a bit of a treat. Mar-

(Above and right) The farmhouse at Gympie.

(Below) 'Sitting Bull', real name Milton, who liked to take it easy when not on the job! And (below, right) the unwelcome visitor found in our outside 'dunny'.

(Above) The centre of Gympie, where I ended up owning a small block of flats as well as a farm.

(Below) Barbara with friends during our visit to Australia in 1984.

(Above) Re-united with childhood sweetheart Barbara in Shipston in 1983 after seventeen years apart, and signing the register at our wedding in 1984.

(Below) Cutting the wedding cake and all dressed up for the local Policeman's Ball.

With brothers Bob (middle) and David (right), family I never knew I had until Bob rang me out of the blue to announce: "You don't know me, but I'm your brother!"

(Opposite) Our double family reunion hits the headlines with (left to right) Barbara, me, brother Bob, my mother Frances, her second husband, Herbert Wood, stepmother 'Wowey', Barbara's daughter Jackie, Bob's wife Sheila and Tiffany.

(Left) Trying to re-create the Aussie outdoor lifestyle in Warwickshire at Great Wolford in 1985.

THE JOURNAL

Incorporating the Cotswold and Cheltenham Journals

No. 6,579   **THURSDAY, JULY 17, 1986**   25p

Your award winning local paper 1st with the

News
Pictures
Sport
Property
Cars
Jobs

THE JOURNAL

Police probe death crash

Police are appealing for witnesses after a man died in an accident in Moreton.

Mr William Shields, 64, of Hospital Road, Moreton, died instantly when he was in collision with a car on the A429 Stow Road at 10.20 p.m. on Saturday.

Neither the driver Mr Allan Preston of Bournemouth nor his passengers were hurt.

Kidney man progressing

Bishops Cleeve window cleaner Derek Keen is making good progress after a kidney transplant operation at Southmead Hospital, Bristol, last week.

Mr Keen, 34, was on holiday in Devon when he got a message that a kidney donor had been found. He refused ambulance assistance and drove himself to the hospital.

Lygon deal is clinched

A £4.85m deal for the worldfamous Lygon Arms Hotel at Broadway has been clinched.

The sale of the 460-year-old country inn to the Savoy Hotel plc went through this week after several months of negotiations.

The Lygon is the Savoy's first country hotel.

Duran Duran star fined

Duran Duran star Roger Taylor was fined £31 by Stow magistrates on Monday for speeding through Moreton.

The 26-year-old, who lives at Little Compton, pleaded guilty by letter but offered no excuses for driving his Land Rover at 51 mph in a 30 mph limit through an endorsement and three points.

Boost for school in shake-up plan

Shipston High School looks set to play a larger part in the community whatever the outcome of the debate over the future of secondary education in South Warwickshire.

The working party looking into the future of secondary schooling last week put forward two proposals, one continuing the present selective system and the other proposing comprehensive education in line with the rest of the county.

Whichever system is eventually adopted Shipston High School's future is guaranteed.

The selective system before council officers for detailed examination and costing includes keeping Shipston as a high school for 11-16 year olds, increasing its intake, and developing it as a community school.

Alternative proposals would establish Shipston as a community college and may necessitate minor changes to its catchment area.

The proposals have been welcomed by Shipston's head Herbert Harpum. "We have always argued that we must look at the full range of facilities on offer if anyone area. This school offers so much to the area, if it were to close there would be no gym, between Stratford and Chipping Norton, no swimming pool and no adult education centre. On the basis of these proposals Shipston school will have a recognised enhanced role in the education and life of the area."

"I am delighted that the future of the school is secure and that the work that has been done here has been recognised."

Among other proposed changes to a comprehensive system Kineton school would become a comprehensive for 11-18 year olds and its range of courses offered to pupils over 16 would be increased with the help of the college of further education.

Relatives shock for childhood sweethearts

Champagne end to family reunion

A family saga to rival the script of any soap opera ended in a huge celebration reunion near Moreton-in-Marsh on Saturday.

It began more than 20 years ago when Barbara Walker and Bernard Byrne became inseparable sweethearts at Shipston High School, drifted apart and Bernard emigrated to Australia.

It has ended with them meeting again, marrying and discovering relations they never knew existed.

Bernard married in Australia but tragedy struck when his wife and two of their young daughters were killed in an horrific car accident, leaving him to bring up four-year-old Tiffany alone.

Barbara also married and while she was expecting her first child, Jonathon

by Angela McLean

and the baby had been adopted. But now Margaret had traced her natural parents and her brothers and sisters.

Barbara admits the news came as a bit of a shock but soon the nerves gave way to delight when the family were reunited at Alf and Edna Walker's home in Todenham.

"We couldn't wait to meet her and now we all get on really well," said Barbara. "Margaret and

Bernard Byrne [...]

On holiday in Portugal.

Barbara's father Alf Walker, pictured in the greengrocer's shop in Shipston that I owned for some years after returning from Australia.

Barbara's daughter, Jackie, in her days as a star hockey player. She helped to cheer me up during a stressful time in my life.

Tiffany and Mark on their wedding day.

(Left) With Tiff and grandchildren Jamie and Chelsie.

Tiff with Jamie and Chelsie.

With the family including (back row) Barbara, Jon, Jackie with baby Ellie, and Tiffany and (front row) me, Jamie and Chelsie.

Back where it all started, with Roy Pool at The Horseshoe in 2006.

garet, the postmistress in Sapphire, kindly supplied the goodies for Santa's sack and a mate of mine, Bernie Wilson, volunteered to dress up as Father Christmas. We took the soft top off the Suzuki, put the windscreen down flat on the bonnet and dressed it up with a bit of festive decoration. Then, after a couple of 'coldies' for Santa and his helper, we drove down to the post office to be greeted by dozens of excited children.

Once the presents had been handed out, Bernie and I adjourned back to his place for a few more cold beers. He was very glad to get out of his Santa outfit as the weather, at least in British terms, was unseasonably hot. Bernie had insisted on wearing the full rig, complete with long pants and boots, which was really very noble of him and way beyond the call of duty. I told him he should have worn shorts and sandals, like all the other Santas in Oz. However, it was a great success and was repeated again the following year.

In the White House, Fay and I enjoyed a happy Christmas with Tiff and Penny and for the first time since arriving in Oz eleven years earlier I was able to look forward with some confidence to a really prosperous New Year. As always at that time of year, my thoughts were clouded with painful memories of Vera, Lou and Kerri, but at least I now seemed to have some sort of future worth living for.

CHAPTER 9

After The Gold Rush

For the next three or four years my mining business continued to flourish and expand.

There were some changes, one of the main ones being that Ted, still having trouble with his back, decided to retire completely and moved down to the Gold Coast, six hundred miles away, where he bought a three-bedroom house just north of Surfers Paradise. At the same time, he also treated himself to a sixteen-foot speedboat in which to go fishing and crabbing.

Although Fay missed having her folks on the doorstep, there was the consolation that we now had a convenient holiday destination, complete with free accommodation and the use of the boat. We went down there whenever we had the opportunity to get away for a few days, setting off at around six in the evening and driving through the night to arrive in time for breakfast the next morning. And while Fay and Edna and the kids stayed on the beach, Ted and I would take the boat out to go fishing along the coast or searching for mud crabs in the mangrove swamps. Some time later, I bought the boat off Ted and brought it back up to the gemfields, where we would take it out to the reservoir at Fairbairn Dam. We'd load up early on a Sunday morning and spend all day there, having barbecues and taking the girls out for joyrides in the boat.

After a while, Jeff also moved down to the coast to be with his parents. Being young and naturally in need of a bit of fun, he found life on the mining fields very boring, with nothing much to do except drink in the bars or go riding his motorbike out in the bush. Even that had had to stop when he came off and broke his arm very badly.

The mate who was with him raced home to raise the alarm and by the time we got to him he was still lying there, crawling with meat ants. He was in hospital for six weeks after that little episode. So, one way and another he'd had enough of Sapphire and as soon as he got a taste of the nightlife down on the coast, that was it.

After he left, his brother John came to work for me instead. He'd bought a caravan, which he parked in my front yard. At around the same time, Ted's two elder boys, Bruce and Ron, who had been living and working down in Inverell for some years, moved back to the mining fields. Bruce rented a house while Ron, who was married with three kids, parked his caravan in the yard outside. Between them, they then bought a magnetic separator, a piece of equipment that separated small sapphires from the ironstone. With this, they were able to make a living by hiring themselves out to the bigger mining outfits.

Later, having also bought themselves a small Traxcavator, they then found a piece of spare ground on Crown Land just west of Sapphire and, although it was illegal to do so, dug out over a thousand yards of dirt one Christmas Eve, a time when they knew that the mining warden would be away on holiday. Using my loader, they then moved the dirt to my plant where we washed it through. We split the proceeds and did quite well out of it, after which we did the same thing on another bit of Crown Land that they found, again working at weekends when we knew that the warden wouldn't be around. This sort of cat-and-mouse activity was going on all the time, so we didn't feel too guilty about it.

Meanwhile, I was continually expanding and upgrading my operation to cope with all the extra work that was coming in. I had a self-feed bin built, to save us having to hose the dirt into the washing plant by hand, and I also bought a little Ferguson tractor and scuttle to facilitate the drying out of the excavated dirt. A second loader and a larger tipper truck helped to speed up the washing process to the rate of two hundred yards-a-day.

Neither the loader nor the truck was taxed. As already mentioned, very few of the miners ever bothered to tax their vehicles because the police rarely came out to the mining fields, except in an emergency.

We used to drink regularly with the local station sergeant and he didn't seem to mind as long as there was no trouble. He was all for a quiet life and as little paperwork as possible.

Things changed, however, when a couple of local tearaways decided to hold up one of the Thai buyers. After robbing him at gun-point, they went on the run out in the bush and soon ended up like modern-day bushrangers, trying to hide out in the barren wastes while a posse of two or three-dozen policemen and trackers from all over the region followed hot on their trail. They managed to evade their pursuers for quite a while but were eventually captured after being surrounded in their camp as they tried to catch some sleep. The pair of them were later sentenced to ten years for armed robbery.

With the law crawling all over the place while this was going on, we were eventually made to tax all our trucks out on the field. This involved driving to Emerald and getting the vehicles inspected for a roadworthiness certificate. Fortunately, I knew the mechanic who tested them and after one or two friendly beers together in the pub across the road and a few minor adjustments, he passed them.

It was shortly after this that I began to think about using some of the money I was making from mining to invest in property. Having grown up on a farm, I had always rather fancied owning one myself one day. During a holiday trip with the family a few years earlier, I'd driven through a town called Gympie, about 120 miles north of Bris-bane, and very much liked the look of the place. I now went down to have another look around and then got in touch with a local estate agent and explained exactly what I was looking for. Before too long, he came up with the ideal property.

A former dairy farm, with an old farmhouse and a collection of wooden outbuildings, it included eighty-five acres on the lower slopes of Mothar Mountain, with a state forest next door. The asking price was A$45,000 – a bargain, I thought. I could put down more than half of that in cash and, with what I had in another account, I could actually afford to pay off almost the whole amount. However, I didn't want to use up all my cash, so I went to see my local bank manager in Emerald and negotiated a loan.

No sooner had that deal been finalised than the agent in Gympie got in touch again to tell me of another forty acres that had come up for sale on the edge of town, just over the hill from the High School, with a very reasonable price tag of just A$20,000. It sounded too good to be true, so we went straight back to Gympie the next weekend to have a look, camping out at the farm, with mattresses thrown down on the floor. As soon as I saw the land, I agreed to buy it on the spot. Now all I had to do was go back to Emerald and explain what I'd done to Pat, the bank manager.

After a solid eight-hour drive, we managed to get back just before closing time on the Monday. As soon as I walked in, with what must have been a rather sheepish grin on my face, Pat looked at me and said: "OK, Bernie. What the hell have you done now?" However, once I had shown him the details of the land and given him a bit of bull, he agreed to loan me the rest of the money. And it turned out to be a fantastic deal, because just over a year later I managed to sell it for A$80,000. With no such thing as capital gains tax in Queensland at that time, this gave me a very healthy profit.

Back in Sapphire, we were keeping so many gems at home by now that we thought it would probably be sensible to have a guard dog around the place. This went down particularly well with Penny and Tiff, who had been on at us for ages to get a dog. We opted for a German Shepherd bitch that we named Shannah. Although she was very good with the kids, she wouldn't let anyone else near the house. Even the Thai buyers who came to see us were wary of her and we had to shut her in the kitchen before they would dare to come in. At the same time, John and his girlfriend Trish, who were still living in the caravan in our yard, also bought a dog – a Doberman that was very stupid and a little unpredictable although, again, very good with the girls. Together, the two dogs certainly looked menacing enough to deter any would-be trespasser.

I was then approached out of the blue a few months later by one of the managers from the nearby Blackwater coal fields, wanting to know if I would be interested in selling The White House. He told me that he was about to retire, but wanted to stay out on the gemfields. I didn't need much persuading when he offered me A$35,000 for the place. After all, it had cost me only A$200 for the plot, plus the cost of the materials I'd had to buy to build the place myself, so I was able to pocket another handsome profit.

Within a month we'd moved out of the house and into a new caravan that I parked on the claim next to Hippie Bruce's place. I soon built a bush shower and toilet, and with air conditioning in the caravan and a concrete floor in the annexe it was almost as comfortable as the house, although obviously not so spacious. John, meanwhile, had moved his caravan onto a claim that his older brother Bruce had managed to acquire.

With our mining operations continuing to tick over very nicely, I decided to put in one last six-blade cut on the claim in the Rush. To my surprise, this went down to a depth of thirty-three feet. Although the dirt was good, this was getting too deep to be economical, what with the hire of the bulldozers alone costing five thousand dollars. Once I'd washed all the dirt from that final cut, I decided it was time to move the plant and ended up buying Bruce's claim, where the excavations had left a pit that filled up during the wet season to form a natural reservoir, providing the water supply that we needed for the washing process. At the same time, I moved our caravan up there, too, and set up camp next to John.

It was now 1981. Throughout the fifteen years that I'd been in Australia I had kept in regular touch with my stepmother, Wowey, though not directly with my father, and I now received a letter from Wowey to say that the old man had been diagnosed with Hodgkinson's Disease. I decided that the time had come to make my first trip back to England since leaving. Although I had never felt at all homesick in all my years away, I was curious to see how things might have changed in my absence and to catch up with family and friends. Apart from that, I knew that Tiff and Penny, both now twelve years old, would enjoy the experience and that Wowey would be thrilled to see Tiff again.

Leaving John to get on with screening and washing a mountain of dirt, I got Jeff to run us down to the airport at Brisbane. I was almost as excited as the girls as we waited to board the jumbo jet, having never done a long-haul flight before. Tiff was actually the most experienced air traveller of us all, having already made the return trip to

England with Vera, although she had been too young then to remember much about it. The first that either of the girls had ever seen of snow was when we were flying over the Alps. A couple of hours later, we touched down at Heathrow at eight o'clock on a crisp October morning.

I'd brought a box of cut stones with me, to show all my friends and relations what we were doing out in Oz. I should have realised that this would cause a bit of difficulty with Customs. After a lot of hassle, I ended up having to pay VAT – a rather unexpected problem since there had been no such thing as VAT when I left England in 1966. We eventually came through the arrivals gate to be met by my father. This was also quite a surprise, as the old man and I had not been on speaking terms since I had walked out on him all those years before. Despite this, he had agreed to let us all stay at the farm and had also volunteered to pick us up at the airport.

Gazing out of the car windows on the way from Heathrow to Harbury, I was immediately struck by just how much England had changed in the time that I had been away. One of the first things I noticed was how much more traffic there was on the roads. And once we got out into the country, I was struck by how relatively barren it looked without all the elm trees, victims of Dutch Elm Disease. Warwickshire was one of the worst-hit counties in this respect, having had so many elms. Once we had settled in at Harbury, I got the old man to let me use his farm van to take Fay and the girls on a tour of the area, including visits to Warwick Castle, Stratford-upon-Avon and the Cotswolds.

Wowey, of course, was overjoyed to see Tiff again, while I found it hard to believe that my little sister, Bridget, who had been about six years old when I left for Australia, was now married, with two sons. But while there had been many changes in my absence, some things were exactly the same. In particular, the relationship between the old man and me remained as strained as ever. It seemed we were still unable to see eye-to-eye and within a fortnight we had a major disagreement, as a result of which I decided to move out of the farm and go down to London for a week or two.

We booked into a hotel and visited all the usual tourist attractions, such as Buckingham Palace, the Tower of London, Big Ben and the Houses of Parliament. We toured in an open-topped, double-decker bus and walked all around the West End and along Oxford Street, looking in all the shop windows. Tiff and Penny loved every minute, having never seen anything quite like it before. We also spent a day with my auntie Maud and uncle Tim, who lived in North London. We took them out to lunch and then, while the women and the girls went shopping again, uncle Tim and I went home to sample some of his home made beer.

We did go back to the farm in Harbury, but after a few days the old man and I managed to fall out yet again and so we returned to London for the last few days before the flight back to Australia. By this time it was getting really cold and we couldn't wait to get back to the sunshine. We flew out on Friday 13th and our flight number was also 13, which perhaps explains why the plane was half-empty. We went via Bahrain, Singapore and Borneo before finally going on down to Brisbane. Right at the end, poor Penny went down with food poisoning and was sick for quite a few days afterwards. Fortunately, the rest of us escaped.

We stayed with Ted and Edna at their place until Penny had fully recovered and then it was back home to Sapphire, where John had been very busy in my absence. Even so, there was still a stack of dirt to be washed and I soon found myself back in the old routine.

Only a week or so after my return, I got a phone call from the agent in Gympie so say that there had been a fire down at the farm and that the house had gone up in smoke, the result, it seemed, of an electrical fault. We got down there to find that the place had been completely gutted and that the whole site was in a terrible mess. Luckily, the bank manager had arranged insurance for us, although this didn't completely cover the cost of rebuilding. I decided to put that job on hold for the time being while I sorted out what I was going to do with the mining business.

Ever since I had bought the farm, I had been thinking of eventually selling up in Sapphire and moving down to Gympie full time. Now that I would have to go down there to rebuild the farmhouse and generally put the place in order, it seemed like a good time to make the change. The perfect opportunity soon arose. After John and I had finished washing the rest of the dirt, I ended up with a large parcel of stone to sell and when I then showed this to Big Smithy and Scottish Jock one evening and mentioned that I was thinking of moving on, they made me an offer for the business. It just so happened that they were looking to buy some more ground for themselves and, as bull-dozing contractors, they had done the last big cut for me, so they were already very familiar with my land. We soon worked out a deal whereby they paid me the same price that I had paid Ted when I bought him out.

I wasted no time in selling off the surplus machinery that I no longer needed before then transporting everything else down to the farm. This involved a couple of trips. First, I loaded up the station wagon and the trailer and took down the bulk of the stuff. I then came back by coach and put the pump and a few other odds and ends on the train, leaving us with just the caravan and the F100 truck. The next day, we said a sad farewell to Sapphire and headed south for a new life down on the farm.

After travelling all day, we got there just before dark. The last part of the journey along a dirt road was a bit hair-raising. With the caravan heavily loaded, my main worry was that we wouldn't be able to get up the steep hill just past the farm owned by our nearest neighbour, Bob Nimmo. It was a matter of getting into first gear and then just going for it. In the end, we just about made it and even then there was still a mile to go to our farm gate.

I parked the caravan right next to one of the sheds, which still had mains electricity connected. During the next few days I managed to fix up a temporary bathroom in the shed and there was also a fairly primitive dunny in the garden. The next job was to clear up the mess of charred timber, fallen masonry and general fire debris that was all that was left of the house. I hired a digger and dumped all the rubbish in a dry gully some distance away. I then got plans drawn up for the new house and started building.

Using a few sub-contractors, I did all the labouring work myself and also operated as site manager, organising the purchase and delivery of all the building materials. The F100 came in very handy for this. We ran out of bricks at one point, so it was off to Cooroy with the trailer in tow and back a few hours later with two tons of bricks. Once again, we only just made it up the hill outside Bob Nimmo's place.

Once the walls were up, the first priority was to finish the loo and put a door on it. The urgent need for a proper toilet had been highlighted when Tiff went down to the dunny in the garden one morning only to emerge, screaming, a few seconds later with the news that there was a big snake in there. Pausing only to grab my rifle, I hurried to investigate and discovered a large and extremely poisonous tiger snake curled up in the roof. I proceeded to blow its head off, but in the process I also blew several holes in the roof. After that little incident there was no way that Fay or the girls would go anywhere near the place.

This was not the first time that they'd had an encounter with a snake in the loo. Back up in Sapphire we came home from a drive-in movie one night to find a half-grown brown snake curled around the base of the lavatory. It must have slithered under the back door in search of somewhere cool to sleep. In that situation, I couldn't use a rifle because of the risk of a ricochet off the tile floor. Instead, I had to despatch it with a broom handle. Even a small snake like that could be deadly if you got bitten and weren't able to get to a hospital quickly enough.

Mothar Mountain, we soon found out, was notorious for its snakes. Apart from the carpet snake – common, but harmless – there were browns, blacks and red-bellied blacks, all extremely venomous. Worst of all were the taipans and death adders. The taipan is the largest of all the snakes found in Australia, with an average length of well over seven-foot. As well as being one of the most poisonous, it is also very aggressive, springing up to strike at the middle of the body. Until the introduction of modern anti-venoms in 1955, more than 90% of taipan bites proved fatal. The death adder, with its unmistakable markings, is smaller but still packs a potentially lethal bite, 50% fatal if not treated with anti-venom.

I encountered all these snakes at various times. Our mail up at the farm was delivered three times-a-week and left in a box up by the farm gate. I went up there on the tractor one lunchtime and came across a six-foot brown laid out across the road, sunning himself. I managed to park the rear wheels of the tractor on him, making sure he couldn't reach up and bite me on the ankles. After wondering for a moment what to do next, I revved the tractor up, put it in reverse and dropped the clutch, and as I shot backwards the snake flew forwards – in three pieces!

If that sounds a bit gruesome, I once saw a television interview with an Australian who was demonstrating the art of snake cracking. He would grab hold of a live snake by the tail and then crack it like a bullwhip, causing its head to fly off! I decided to stick with the rifle or the shotgun!!

With so many snakes about, our greatest fear was for the children. They would ride their bikes a mile up the track to catch the school bus and would quite often see snakes. Anxious that they might get bitten, I got on to the education authority and tried to persuade them to let the bus come up the track to the house, but they refused to go that extra mile.

In addition to the farm, I had invested in another property in Gympie shortly before we left Sapphire. Using the handsome A$60,000 profit from the sale of the extra forty acres on the edge of town that I had acquired at the same time as the farm, I invested in a small block of six flats. The rent I got from these flats kept us going financially until I was able to get the farm up and running to the point where it was paying its own way.

My first move was to establish a herd of beef cattle. To help me rebuild the farmhouse, I had brought in a carpenter, Mick Thatcher, who was also a farmer and he was able to help me get started. He was running a beef suckler herd, but had decided to switch from Herefords to a tropical breed and he therefore agreed to sell me the pick of his Herefords.

I went out to his place one Saturday morning and we saddled up a couple of the stock ponies that he also bred before riding out together to round up the cattle. Mick's property was spread over more than fifteen hundred acres and the herd could have been anywhere, so the best way to find them was to turn cowboy. It was the first time I'd been on a horse for about twelve years. The girls had certainly never seen me on one before and they were quite surprised when I jumped into the saddle and rode off with Mick.

It took us a couple of hours to find the herd and drive them back to the yard. After a barbecue lunch and a few coldies it was then time to sort out what I wanted. I first picked out Milton, the best bull, and ended up with fifty-four Hereford cows and their calves, plus one Jersey cow that was also in calf. With my eighty-five acres, plus the free grazing up on the side of Mothar Mountain, I would have more than enough grass for that number and with five spring-fed dams on the farm there would also be plenty of water for them, even during dry spells.

I hired a local carrier to transport them over to my spread and had the whole lot there by the next day. They went mad when first let out of the truck, stampeding around all over the place. However, they soon settled down and established their regular daily grazing pattern, so that I knew exactly where they would be at any given time.

I had fixed up all the boundary fences beforehand, Bob kindly allowing me to cut ironbark posts from a convenient patch of scrub on his neighbouring property. It was simply a matter of felling a few of the right-sized trees and towing them home with the Ferguson tractor that I'd brought with me from Sapphire. I had renewed the stockyard enclosure in the same way.

Looking after the whole herd single-handed was quite a job. I had to bring them in every eighteen days to spray them for ticks and, in between, there was the usual cutting, branding and de-horning to keep me busy. I'd bought a sprayer to go on the back of the tractor for the spraying of the groundsel that grew all over the property and I used the same equipment to spray the cattle. Once I'd got them corralled in the stockyard, they would just stand there or amble around contentedly while I did the job, looking as though they thoroughly enjoyed a cooling shower. There was only one cow that was bad-tempered and she was always treated first and then put back outside the yard, by herself.

Once the rebuilding of the house was complete, I bought more machinery and started ploughing up some ground ready to grow small crops of vegetables. I started with two acres of French beans, but just as they were coming along nicely a few hares got in one night and ate all the shoots. I had to fence the whole area with chicken wire before replanting. With this protection, I grew a very successful crop the second time around, only to find that picking the beans was a backbreaking job. Having decided that tomatoes and cucumbers would be easier, I built a few frames outside one of the sheds and put in about three thousand seeds in pots. Under protest, Tiff and Penny helped plant the tomato seeds, their smaller fingers being ideal for this rather fiddly job. After a couple of days I looked in the frames to find that this time it was the mice that had got in, digging up and eating a lot of the seeds. Again, I had to make the frames mouse-proof before re-planting the whole lot.

Despite these minor setbacks, I soon managed to get the vegetable side of the business up and running properly. The water pump that had done such good service in the washing plants up in the gemfields now proved just as effective in helping to irrigate the vegetable plots during the dry season, pumping water down from the main dam. Before too long I was not only selling my produce locally in Gympie, but also sending regular daily consignments to the Brisbane markets by train.

With the cattle and the vegetables between them providing me with a decent income, I was really getting to enjoy my new life as a farmer. It may not have been quite as lucrative as mining, but the routine and the lifestyle was more to my liking and the environment was vastly superior.

There were two old mango trees at one end of the farmhouse and I would sit out there with a beer most evenings, looking down on the main dam and watching the wildlife. Apart from the wild ducks that would fly in at that time of day, you could sometimes, if you were lucky and kept your eyes peeled, catch sight of the duck-billed platy-puses that came up from Six Mile Creek, about half-a-mile away, to swim around and play in the water.

There were also freshwater crayfish in most of the dams. Their tell-tale mud holes could be seen around the edges of the water and the best way to catch them was to poke a thin stick down the holes to stir up the water and make it muddy. This would cause them to come out and once they poked their two long whiskers out of the water you had to drive a spade underneath them at an angle, so that they couldn't retreat back into their holes. You could then reach down and grab them. As well as being very good to eat, they also made excellent bait for fishing in the local creeks and rivers.

Bob, next door, was a keen sea angler and when the timing was right he and I would go out together to fish the night tide. This being the Pacific Ocean, you could catch all sorts of stuff and I bought myself a sea rod and reel that I used with an eighty-pound line, just in case I hooked something really big.

One night, when we hadn't done very well, we decided to go back to the mouth of the Noosa River, at the point where the estuary flows into the sea. Fishing from a jetty there, it wasn't long before I felt a massive tug on the end of my line. Unfortunately, after playing the fish for several minutes, the eighty-pound line snapped, so I never did find out what I had hooked. Whatever it was, it must have been very big, probably a shark.

The biggest thing either of us ever caught was a sixteen-pound sea dew that Bob bagged. One of his mates was always taking the Mickey out of him about how he never caught anything decent so, even though it was after midnight, Bob insisted on going straight round to his house to wake him up and show off this prize trophy, which he placed in the kitchen sink. He never had any more ribbing after that.

Meanwhile, Ted was tired of living on the coast and was missing the bush, so he put his house at Surfers Paradise up for sale. At the same time, he spotted a seven-acre plot that he rather fancied at Pie Creek, on the other side of Gympie from us. I had a few dollars to spare, so I loaned him the deposit while he waited for his place to be sold. Once the money came through, he intended to build a new house for himself on the plot and, in the meantime, he and Edna moved into our caravan at the farm.

While he was waiting, he and I started going over to the plot to fence it and also to plant some trees and a patch of grapevines. He even bought an old Howard rotovator with which to prepare the ground – but because of his bad back that ended up being my job!

His plans were then somewhat disrupted by a drop in property prices that caused the housing market to go very quiet, with the result that he couldn't immediately sell the house at Surfers Paradise. In fact, it was to be two years before a buyer was found. After two months, he got fed up with travelling to and fro between the farm and Pie Creek and asked if he could move the caravan up there so that he could live on the site. I certainly had no objection and helped him to rig up a temporary bush shower and a toilet. With electric power supplied by a generator left over from our mining days, he and Edna were soon quite comfortably settled in.

Just before they moved, Ted and I had bought a dozen fat lambs between us. I made a special crate for the F100 so that we could bring them home from market. We kept them at the farm and slaughtered and butchered them as and when we needed the meat. This made a welcome change from the steak that we ate most of them time as a result of having our own beef cattle herd. What with the fish that I was catching in Six Mile Creek and in Gympie's Mary River, along with all the fresh vegetables that I was growing and fruit from the trees that I had planted, we were now pretty much self-sufficient. And with the rent from the flats supplementing the income from the farm, we were fairly well off.

But then, just when it seemed that life was settling into a comfortable routine once again, another drama intervened to spark a chain of events that was to turn everything completely upside down.

CHAPTER 10

Full Circle

In 1983, after nearly ten long years of seemingly endless legal wran-
gling, a date was at last set for a high court hearing at Narrabri in New
South Wales at which a judgement was to be delivered in the compensation case arising out of the accident.

Accompanied by Fay and the girls, along with Ted and Edna, I travelled down the day before to meet with my barrister, who had flown
in from Sydney – at my expense, of course!

The court appearance was scheduled for ten o'clock the next
morning, but at the last moment we were told that a rape case involving three Aboriginals had been held over from the day before and
would have to be dealt with first. It wasn't until after lunch that we
were called back into the courtroom to be informed that the barris-
ters on either side wanted to settle out of court. The judge, too,
seemed to be in favour of this, so I felt I had no option but to go along
with it.

As mentioned earlier, the sum they eventually agreed on was just
A$25,000 of which A$4,000 immediately went to pay the legal fees
involved while $5,000 went into a trust fund for Tiff. As far as I was
concerned, no amount of money could ever compensate for what I
had lost, but, even so, I couldn't help thinking that it was a rather
inadequate sum given the enormity of what had happened. But I
guess that's what you have to expect when an individual goes up
against a big company.

Far from being a benefit in any way, the money turned out to be
curse that helped only to poison my relationship with Fay, causing
further totally unexpected misery and upheaval in my life.

Fay and I had been going through a rather rocky patch for some weeks before the court hearing. I couldn't really work out what the problem was. We'd had a pretty good life in the mining fields and, as far as I was concerned, things were even better down on the farm. We were making money there and we had the additional income from the flats. We also had more time to ourselves and could afford to go away wherever we wanted at weekends, which we often did. So what was wrong? She didn't really seem to have an answer apart from saying that she wanted to 'do her own thing', as she put it.

The trouble really started almost immediately after the court hearing when Fay made it clear that she thought she should be entitled to half the compensation award. When I made it equally clear that I saw no reason to hand it over to her, she quickly became very bitter and, as things rapidly deteriorated, it wasn't long before everybody started taking sides. Ted, to whom I had actually loaned part of the compensation award so that he could pay off the balance of what he owed for the land at Pie Creek, was clearly embarrassed by what was going on and warned his daughter to behave properly, but she took absolutely no notice of him.

Edna, meanwhile, lined up with Fay and suddenly began turning up at the farm to take her out 'shopping'. I became suspicious after a while and started asking questions about what they were actually up to on these expeditions, but that only made things worse and I ended up having cups of hot coffee thrown at me. At the same time, as I found out later, Fay had been doing her best to turn Tiff against me.

She chose my 38th birthday as the moment to move out of the farm and into one of the flats we owned, taking both Penny and Tiff with her. I would go in every day to see the girls, taking them fruit and vegetables. Meanwhile, Ted and Edna only came out to the farm when they wanted something, usually free vegetables. When I eventually put a stop to Edna coming round and helping herself to my beans for her freezer, that was it – I never saw anything more of them after that.

Soon after Fay moved out, I received a letter from her solicitor. It seemed she wanted to sell me out and take half of everything, plus half of my share as 'maintenance' for the girls. I was horrified. I suddenly had to face the fact that everything I had worked so hard for over eighteen years was about to be taken away from me, and it seemed there was nothing I could do about it. The law was on her side and even though we weren't married, it seemed she was indeed entitled to half of everything – the house, the farm, the flats…the lot.

Meanwhile, Tiff and Penny were at High School, growing up fast and old enough to have minds of their own. They could see exactly what was going on in the flats and reported back to me with a few tales about Fay's behaviour that I found quite alarming.

I was soon left in no doubt that she was intent on taking me for every penny I'd got. I was in Gympie one day doing a bit of shopping when I bumped into one of Mick Thatcher's daughters. She was hobbling around on crutches having fallen off a horse up at his farm, breaking her leg. We went and had a coffee and as we were chatting the subject of conversation turned to my mining days and she expressed an interest in seeing some of the sapphires that I'd had cut and had kept for myself. As we happened to be just down the road from the bank where I kept them in a safe deposit box, I went and got them out to show her. Afterwards, when I returned them, I made sure that they were registered under my name alone. This turned out to have been a very good move on my part since the next thing I heard was that Fay had been in not long after that, trying to get hold of them for herself.

I was at a very low ebb when, three months after she had moved out of the farm, something happened that, looking back later, seemed like destiny. Suddenly, right out of the blue, I got a letter from Barbara Walker, my childhood sweetheart from all those years ago in Shipston. It had been addressed to me c/o the Post Office in Sapphire and had been sent on by Ron, who was still working up there.

In the letter, Barbara explained that she had suddenly found herself thinking about me, wondering whatever had happened to me and what I was doing and had decided that she would try to get in touch. She had managed to get the Sapphire address from Wowey, but had then had second thoughts about whether it was the right thing to do. It was another year before she actually got around to writing, by which time I had moved to Gympie.

She wanted to know if I still remembered her and I wrote back straightaway saying that of course I did, mentioning the colour of her eyes, her middle name, her parents' first names and even the names of the pony and the dog she used to have when we were at school together. I also told her about Vera and the kids and brought her right up-to-date with my life, including my troubles with Fay.

Within a matter of days I had a reply, saying that she, too, was separated, although still in business with her husband, Mick Williams, and that she had two children, a son and a daughter, who were living with her on a small farm just outside Shipston. Hearing from Barbara again after all those years was just the lift in life that I needed after all the hassle and worry of the previous few months. From then on, we started writing to each other every week.

In the meantime, Fay was getting more and more difficult and was especially incensed when I let it drop that I was in touch with an old flame from the past. Since it was she who had walked out on me, I didn't feel in the least bit guilty about that.

As the rows got worse and worse, I visited the flat less and less, although I did still manage to speak to the girls on a regular basis. They, it seemed, were not speaking to Fay that much by this time. Threatening her solicitor didn't do me much good, I know, but it made me feel better when, at one point, he ran out of his office to avoid having to confront me.

An agent was duly appointed and the farm was put up for sale. I tried to run it down as much as I could in an effort to put people off and postpone the inevitable. This worked for a while and the first few people who came to view the place took one look and went away again. But then, eventually, a serious buyer came along and offered the asking price, leaving me with no option but to sign it away.

I was heartbroken. In so many ways, those few acres represented the fulfilment of all my dreams. Coming so soon after the conclusion of the compensation case, which had forced me to live through the trauma of the accident once again, re-awakening terrible memories, this was an even more crushing blow than it would have been anyway. It really got me down.

Fay, meanwhile, became ever more relentless in her quest to screw every last penny out of me. She decided she wanted half the cattle and half the machinery from the farm. I was equally determined that she was not going to get either, but I had to act quickly. First, I got hold of a local agent who sold all the cattle for me. I then got a mate of mine to bring out a truck and remove all the machinery, hiding it somewhere where I knew she would never find it.

The couple that had bought the farm were eager to move in, having already sold their previous property, and by December 14th contracts had been signed and the deal was moving swiftly towards completion. At this point I made a spur-of-the-moment decision to fly back to England for Christmas. As well as writing to each other, Barbara and I had also spoken on the phone by this time and I had already talked about going back to see her in England at some stage in the very near future, without actually naming a date. Now, having hurriedly booked a flight, I sent a telegram to say that I would be arriving at Heathrow on Christmas Eve.

Two days before flying out, I moved into one of the flats in Gympie, taking with me what was left of the furniture at the farm. I checked with the girls that they didn't mind me jetting off to England and they were fine about it. They were looking forward to the summer holidays and I suspected that they both had boyfriends that they were meeting down at the swimming pool, so no doubt had other things on their minds!

I went to see my solicitor and gave him power of attorney so that he could authorise more money to be sent over to me if I needed it. I had no option but to leave the flats in Fay's hands while I was away, a very costly mistake, as it later turned out. After saying goodbye to the girls, I jumped on the coach and headed for the airport at Brisbane. By the time I got there, it was so hot that it was a relief just to sit in the air-conditioned departure lounge, sipping an ice-cold beer as I waited to board the 3pm flight. Even though I knew it was midwinter in England, it was hard to imagine at that point just how different the temperature would be when I stepped off the plane at Heathrow!

Our route took us first to Singapore and then to Bahrain, where my end of the aircraft was invaded by a party of eight very merry Geordies, oilfield workers on their way back to England for Christmas. That was when the party started and for the next seven hours it was non-stop singing and drinking all the way.

I came down to earth with a bang. It was still dark outside as I emerged shivering and somewhat bleary-eyed into the arrivals hall at Heathrow at seven o'clock on a freezing cold morning and became acutely aware that I was not really dressed for the English winter. All I had on was a singlet, a shirt and a thin pair of trousers. On my feet was the only pair of proper shoes I owned, bought just before I left Australia. Over there, I only ever wore sandals and actually went around barefoot most of the time.

I was met at the airport by Pete, my sister Bridget's husband at the time, and their two sons, Colin and Ben, who were then nine and seven respectively. I was going to be staying with them, as I was once again not on speaking terms with the old man following our falling-out on the previous visit. As soon as I got to their place, I rang Barbara. Being Christmas Eve, she was working flat out in the shop she owned with her husband in Moreton-in-Marsh and couldn't get away, but we agreed to meet on Boxing Day. In the meantime, I spent a rather jet-lagged Christmas Day with Bridget, Pete and Wowey, who had come over without the old man.

The following morning at ten o'clock Barbara pulled up outside the house in her Range Rover. Still suffering the effects of jet lag, I was running late and had only just got out of the shower when she arrived. I was so excited about seeing her that I couldn't wait to get dressed properly, but raced straight out to greet her, barefoot and wearing just a singlet and trousers.

After a kiss and cuddle we went inside and I don't know which of us was the more nervous. We both agreed that we had not changed that much in the eighteen years since we had last seen each other, although Barb admitted that she was quite envious of the deep tan I had acquired through working outdoors in the hot Aussie sun most of time.

There was an awful lot of catching up to be done and after the initial introductions had been made, Bridget and Pete, along with Wowey, beat a hasty retreat to Pete's mother's house, leaving us alone for the rest of the day – and night! We talked non-stop until about seven in the evening when, still tired from the long trip over, I began to flag a bit. With Barb's mum looking after her two kids it seemed only natural that we should collapse onto the bed and cuddle up for the night. That didn't last long! We were awake again by midnight and talking again. I think we finally got to sleep at about four in the morning.

Barb had to return to work the next day, as she had the shop to run, but she came back on New Year's Eve, this time with her kids, Jackie and Jon. We had Pete and Bid's flat to ourselves as they were staying at his mum's house while she was away in Germany for a few days' holiday. Very shortly afterwards they were joined there by Wowey. She was finding the old man more and more difficult to live with and, as a result, had finally made up her mind to leave him for good. I went over to Harbury to explain to him what was going on and, needless to say, he didn't take kindly to what I had to tell him. Sadly, that was to be the last time I ever spoke to him.

After all this, I was having to think seriously about whether I was going to stay in England or go back to Australia and it didn't take me long to decide that I would remain in England, at least for the time being. Since separating from her husband, Barb had been lodging with an old friend of hers, Nigel Ridout, who owned a farm and riding stable just outside Shipston, and he now offered the two of us a room there. At the same time, he wanted four more stables built and, with the building experience I had gained in Australia, this was an easy job for me to get on with. I had them up in no time.

Meanwhile, I was getting a lot of angry letters from Fay in Australia. She maintained that she couldn't manage on the money she had and announced that, because of this, she had decided to keep all the rent from the flats. It had been agreed that the block should be put up for sale, but she was careful to put off any prospective buyers. With all the rent, plus the social security benefits she had managed to claim, she was sitting pretty, thank you very much; and being 12,000 miles away, there was not an awful lot I could do about it.

Much more upsetting as far as I was concerned was the suspicion that she was again doing her best to turn Tiff against me in my absence. This came through very clearly in the letters I got from Tiff herself. I found this very upsetting, because I was already only too well aware that if I did decide to stay permanently in England, this would cause all sorts of complications in her life. Mel and Beryl, the couple from whom I had bought the flats, were keeping me informed about the situation out there and assured me that she and Penny were both back at school and coping very well, but this was obviously a problem I would have to address before too long.

Anxiety about Tiff's future and uncertainty about my own, combined with the strain of trying to sort out my affairs in Australia while dealing with all the long-distance aggravation from Fay, were beginning to have a serious effect on my health and for several months I found myself very much under the weather, both physically and psychologically. The truth of the matter was that although the euphoria of getting back together with Barbara had helped to take my mind off things, I had already been in a bit of a state when I came back from Australia. And once the initial excitement had died down after Christmas and I faced up to the realities of my situation in the cold, grey light of an English winter I felt severely stressed. It came as no great surprise when I was diagnosed with an ulcer and put on some fairly heavy medication. It was to be some time before I got myself properly straightened out.

Despite all the nagging worries, I was gradually becoming more and more settled back in England. In March, a small cottage came up for sale in Todenham, a village between Shipston and Moreton-in-Marsh, not far from where Barbara and I were living on Nigel's farm. I bought it, using the money from the sale of the farm in Gympie, and did it up with the intention of living there, at least for the time being. But then, even before we'd had a chance to move in, a very nice bungalow with more than four acres of land came on the market in the neighbouring village of Great Wolford. I took Barb to see it and the look on her face said it all: this was a place where she could be very happy. Not only would it be ideal for Jackie and Jon, but with all that land we could also have animals there and I could even grow a few vegetables.

Until I was able to get my hands on the proceeds from the sale of the flats in Australia, the only problem was money. Fortunately, however, I was able to arrange a bridging loan to tide me over. At the same time, I got a job with the farmer next door. Andrew Wrench had a dairy herd and a fair number of pigs up at Mount Sorrell and as well as needing a hand to look after them, he also wanted help with some building work he had planned. Obviously, I was his man! And it suited me because I needed to make a bit of money to pay for my air fare back to Aussie, where I intended to sort out the flats and one or two other business matters once and for all.

Before that, however, there was one other little matter that I wanted to attend to. I had bought a box of my sapphires back with me from Oz and, without telling Barbara, I had picked out the best one and had it set in an engagement ring for her. Having gone into Stratford secretly to pick it up one afternoon, I was still out when Barb came back from working in the shop and she admitted to me later that when she got back and found me missing she thought for a moment that I'd done a runner and had gone back to Australia. When I did eventually put in an appearance an hour or two later and presented her with the ring she immediately accepted my proposal. So, we were now officially engaged. Barb's divorce from Mick having been finalised, we announced that the wedding would take place that September.

In the meantime, there was more and more work to be done for Andrew up at Mount Sorrell. People were quite amazed to see me running around everywhere barefoot, even when we were doing the concreting and other heavy building work. I just wasn't used to wearing shoes, although I did put on a pair of wellies when it came to mucking out the pigs!

That summer of 1984 was one of the hottest for years and Barbara's brother, Reg Walker, was more in demand than ever for the pig roasts that he was famous for organising throughout the area. A larger-than-life character in his cowboy hat and red neckerchief, Reg regularly took me along to give him a hand on these occasions, his sunny nature and sense of fun always helping to cheer me up in those early months after my return to the UK when I still felt under a lot of pressure because of the situation I'd left behind in Australia.

Someone else who helped to get me through that stressful period was Barb's daughter, Jackie. She was only eight or nine years old at the time and she could be a right cheeky little monkey, always up to mischief, but she used to keep me amused with her antics. As a birthday present, Barbara had given me a Jack Russell pup that we christened Saff – as in Sapphire – and when it came to bath time, Jackie would always insist on sticking Saff in the tub to give her a bath, too, which would always cause absolute havoc. With this lively little girl around, a smile was never very far away. She went on to become a top class county hockey player with Warwickshire and also an England international trialist, coached by Olympic star Jill Sixsmith.

As Barb and I settled into the bungalow at Great Wolford during that first, heatwave summer of 1984, one of my early priorities was to build a barbecue so that I could show our friends what the Aussie lifestyle was like. At the same time, I was gradually managing to adjust back to life in England. The highlight of the summer was, of course, the wedding. Barb and I had been getting on so well and were so happy together from the moment that we were re-united – it was as if we had both been given a wonderful new lease of life. The wedding took place in the local register office in Shipston and afterwards there was a small reception party out at the bungalow.

We didn't go away for a honeymoon right away because by now we had decided that we would both go to Australia together to sort out all my unfinished business with Fay and also to try and work out what was going to happen with Tiff.

Barb had never flown before and became increasingly nervous as the moment of departure approached. We had arranged for Wowey to come and stay at the bungalow to look after Jackie and Jon as well as the chickens that we were keeping by this time. The eggs had to be collected, graded and boxed before being sent up to Barb and Mick's shop in Moreton.

On the big day, we were at the railway station at Moreton at the crack of dawn, ready to catch the first train to Paddington before then going on by bus to Heathrow. Our flight wasn't due to leave until nine o'clock that night, but we wanted to give ourselves plenty of time, even if it meant sitting around the airport all day. I could see when we got there that Barb was becoming more and more anxious and worked up, so I thought it would be a good idea if we had a few drinks while we waited, just to calm her nerves. By the time we boarded the aircraft we'd downed about ten whiskies and were both pretty relaxed as a result.

I knew that once dinner had been served on the plane we would be able to settle down for about five hours' kip before we landed in Bahrain. As it happened, Barb was fine through take-off and during most of the flight but started to feel poorly as soon as we began our descent into Bahrain. After swallowing a couple of pills given to her by a stewardess she felt a bit better and was fine by the time we actually landed, but the same thing happened at the next stop-off in Singapore and we were both mightily relieved when we finally touched down safely in Brisbane. Here Barb experienced the pleasant surprise of stepping out of the plane at the start of the Australian summer, having got into it as winter set in back home in England. It was only seven o'clock when we arrived, but the temperature was already about 70°. We both like the heat, so this was pure heaven.

Once we had cleared customs, we went straight off to the best hotel in Brisbane for a couple of days rest and relaxation before going on up to Gympie. At the Crest, we showered and then crashed out for a couple of hours – just long enough to refresh ourselves but not so long as to make the jet lag worse by putting ourselves completely out of kilter with the time difference.

It was mid-afternoon when we came to again and we decided to go walkabouts in the city centre. Brisbane is such a clean-looking, friendly place, with one-way streets laid out on a grid system. All the streets going in one direction have boys' names, while all those in the other direction are named after girls, making it very easy to get around. Barb loved it from the word go and we explored most of the city centre and located all the most important shops in those first few hours. After a solid night's sleep, the next day was then spent shopping, mostly for clothes. Barb needed some summer dresses and, most importantly, a bikini and a swimsuit, while I just went for my usual Aussie 'uniform' of shorts and singlets.

We had already phoned Mel and Beryl to announce our arrival – which caught them completely by surprise – and we now called them again to let them know that we would be coming up to Gympie by bus the following day. Once we got out of Brisbane, the two-and-a-half-hour journey took us through some wonderful countryside, an area that produces tropical fruit such as pineapple, banana, Kiwi and passion fruit, paw-paw and orange as well as a whole range of vegetables including pumpkins, squashes, tomatoes, chokos and many more. When I had first arrived there many years before there had also been a lot of tobacco plantations, but these seemed to have largely disappeared.

We arrived in Gympie at lunchtime and Barb was amazed at the size of the place. Because there is so much space available, towns in Australia tend to spread out rather than up and Gympie is sprawled over quite a few square miles. Mel was there to meet us off the coach and drove us out to his place, which was about three miles from the town centre, next to a pine forest. Again, Barb fell in love with it – and was especially impressed by the orange and lemon trees and the banana plants in his back garden.

We sat out on Mel's verandah until late in the evening, chatting away over a few drinks and occasionally breaking off to watch the many spiders that were busy constructing their webs up in the rafters. At the same time, frogs and crickets provided a continuous soundtrack in the background, croaking and chirping away for all they were worth. For a few relaxing hours, I was reminded of all the things I liked best about the Aussie lifestyle.

I was brought down to earth with a jolt the next day when the now all-too-familiar hassles with Fay began again. She had heard that I was back in town and from then on she was constantly on the phone, giving me all sorts of grief about the flats and everything else she could think of to complain about. There were times when she would start banging on to such an extent that I would simply hang the phone on the wall and go back to sit on the verandah while she carried on. I'd go back about twenty minutes later and she would still be babbling away. Eventually, I would say a few choice words and hang up.

We had another prospective buyer lined up for the flats, but once again Fay was being difficult. This time I felt I had to go and give her a public warning, as it were. If she didn't agree to sell, I told her, I would have her kicked out and the entire matter would be put in the hands of the solicitors to sort out.

While all this was going on, Penny and Tiff seemed to be perfectly happy doing their own thing. At this stage I had not yet mentioned that my plan was to take Tiff back to England with me, wanting to wait for the right moment to broach that difficult subject

In the meantime, I needed to get Barb away from all the bickering and arguing – after all, this was supposed to be our honeymoon! So, Mel having kindly offered me the use of his Ford Fairlaine for a few days, I arranged a surprise trip down to Coolum Beach where I had booked into the Alamanda Hotel, overlooking the beach and the Pacific Ocean. The beach itself stretches for about twelve miles, from Coolum right up to Noosa, and apart from the odd fisherman, it was virtually deserted most of the time. We spent some very happy hours strolling along the sands or relaxing beside the hotel pool.

This peaceful interlude was ended by a phone call from Mel to say that a definite buyer for the flats had been found and that we should return to Gympie straightaway to make sure everything went through without any further interference from Fay. No sooner had we arrived back at Mel's than she appeared, with smoke and flames coming out of her nostrils, or so it seemed to me. Mel and I were in his garage sorting out some of my tools and equipment from the farm when she came storming in and launched straight into another tirade, even threatening at one point to club me with my own branding iron before eventually calming down enough to accept that the flats had to be sold.

Once the dust had settled and we were able to have a vaguely sensible conversation, she revealed that she had bought Ted and Edna's house down on the Gold Coast and was planning to move out there as soon as the sale of the flats was finalised, taking the girls with her. Tiff, who had been with her when she came raging into Mel's garage and had witnessed that final shouting match, was understandably confused by it all and decided that she wasn't ready to fly back with Barb and me right away, needing time to get things sorted out in her own mind. Instead, it was agreed that she would stay on at school for the time being and come over to England later.

With everything now more or less settled, Barb and I headed back to Coolum to enjoy a few more days of peace and tranquillity at the Alamanda before preparing to fly home. Despite the aggravation with Fay, it had been a fantastic trip for both of us, but especially for Barb, who was seeing Australia for the first time and for whom it was all a great new adventure.

Mel and Beryl had been fantastic in every way and we'd had some great relaxing times with them. There had been barbecues out in the bush, including one at the Barumba Dam, where Barb was enchanted when she got a tame Kookaburra to feed from her hand. We had made visits to a pineapple farm and other tourist attractions and had even enjoyed a spot of fishing – Beryl always being the one to catch the most. These were happy days, indeed – days that we will both remember for the rest of our lives.

When the time eventually came to say goodbye, Mel saw us off on the coach from Gympie to Brisbane, where we still had two days to spare before the flight home. I was determined to make the most of them and, apart from sightseeing and shopping, I took Barbara to the Lone Pine Koala Sanctuary, just up the river from the city, where she was able to cuddle koalas, stroke kangaroos and see some of Australia's other wildlife at close quarters. She wasn't quite so keen on the snakes and lizards!

We had our last supper in the restaurant at the Crest Hotel and then, all too soon, it was time to head for the airport and the flight home. As we took off and I looked down out of the cabin window, knowing that this could be the last I would ever see of Australia, I was overwhelmed with feelings of nostalgia, tinged with great sadness for what I was leaving behind. I had, after all, had eighteen years of the most extraordinary adventures here on the other side of the world and although I hadn't exactly made my fortune, I had certainly achieved more than I ever could have done if I'd settled for a life down on the farm in Warwickshire. At the same time, I had suffered a terrible and tragic loss for which nothing could ever make up. But at least I had been left with Tiff – and now I had Barb, too. So, there was new hope for the future.

As the ground receded into the distance beneath me before finally vanishing out of sight altogether, I was reminded of that day in 1966 when I had stood on the deck of the Fairsea, watching the coast of England disappearing over the horizon and wondering what lay ahead of me. The wheel had now come full circle in the most unexpected way and I was heading back to a future that was still uncertain but that was also full of promise once again.

Epilogue

I was twenty-one years old when I left England for Australia. And more than twenty-one years have now passed since I came back for good in 1984 to start a new life with Barbara in Warwickshire.

After everything that I had been through Down Under, I count myself very fortunate to have been given another chance to find love and happiness. The extraordinary circumstances that led me right back to where I started from, and to the childhood sweetheart I'd left behind all those years before, had already made mine a remarkable story. But there was still another incredible twist to come. A double twist, in fact.

I was sitting at home in Great Wolford one Sunday afternoon in 1985, watching the farming programme on television, when the telephone rang.

"Hello, is that Bernie Byrne?" asked a voice that I didn't recognise.

"It is," I said. "Who's calling?"

"It's your brother, Bob," came the reply.

My first thought was that it must be my mate Geoff Turner, trying to take the Mickey.

"OK, p*** off, Turner!" I said. "You know I don't have a brother."

"Listen, I'm serious," insisted the caller. "I know that this will come as a bit of a shock to you, since you have obviously never been aware that I existed, but I really am your brother."

My mouth fell open as he went on to explain that I had also got another brother, David, not to mention five half-bothers and half-sisters and a stepsister!

I listened in amazement as he proceeded to tell me the whole story of how my mother, Frances, had not been killed in the war, as my father had always maintained, but had simply walked out on him, taking Bob and David with her but leaving me behind for some reason that has never quite been explained. Even when I was eventually re-united with Frances, who has since died, she couldn't remember the details – or maybe she just didn't want to. She was very guarded and clearly had no desire to talk about that part of her life. Perhaps the memories were just too painful.

As for me, I found it very difficult to think of her as my mother. Obviously, I had been curious to meet her and to find out what she was like, but I was uncertain and a little apprehensive in advance about what my feelings towards her might be. As it turned out, there was no great natural bond between us after all those years. It was like being introduced to a very distant relation, all rather low key and unemotional. And after that first re-union we just drifted apart again and never saw that much of each other.

On the other hand, I was delighted to be re-united with Bob and David, with whom I have remained close ever since and get on with very well indeed. Both now retired, Bob was the Head Supervisor for the North Staffordshire Ambulance Service and lives with his wife, Sheila, in Derrington in Staffordshire, while David was a farmer. He and his wife, Margaret, now live near Uttoxeter. Bob has two sons by his first marriage – James and Anthony – and David and Margaret also have a son, Andrew, so I had three nephews to add to the two half-brothers (Phil and Paul), three half-sisters (Frances, Helen and Frieda) and one stepsister (Connie) that I had acquired as a result of Frances' marriage to Herbert Wood.

What made the sudden appearance of this large new family even more remarkable was that not very long beforehand, by some quite extraordinary co-incidence, Barbara, too, had been shocked to discover that she had a sister and a half-sister that she had never known she had.

Her sister Margaret had been born when her parents, Alf and Edna Walker, were still in their teens and, as a result, the baby had been put up for adoption. Taking advantage of a change in the law that had previously protected the identity of an adopted child's real parents, Margaret had managed to trace Alf and Edna and had eventually been re-united with them.

The story of this double family re-union made the front page of our local Newspaper, The Journal, with me pictured cracking a bottle of champagne in celebration, together with my mother and my brother Bob, Barb and her sister Margaret and various other members of the two families.

Afterwards, Barb remarked jokingly to her mum: "Now, tell me – you haven't got any more surprises like that up your sleeve, have you?"

"Oh, no," promised Edna. "Absolutely not!" But the words were hardly out of her mouth before a half-sister, Shirley, suddenly materialised, the result of a relationship between Alf and a girlfriend, Molly.

One way and another, our lives seemed to be turning into some rather far-fetched soap opera!

Only a few weeks before the story of these family re-unions made front-page news in July 1986, Tiff had at last returned from Australia to live with Barb and me and Barb's two children, Jackie and Jon. Although a bit bewildered when it was first suggested that she should come back to England with us and understandably rather reluctant to make the move, she had subsequently come to realise that there wouldn't be much of a future for her with Fay.

Once it had become clear that I wouldn't be going back to Aussie, Fay started to take her bitterness out on Tiff instead, things eventually getting so bad that Tiff actually ran away to seek refuge with Ted and Edna. Penny had already left home and had gone to live with friends in Roma by this time, while Fay had given birth to another child, Nathan, by a new partner. When Fay discovered that Tiff was in regular touch with me she went completely berserk for some reason and it was then that Tiff decided the time had come to get out. She fled the house one morning and set out to walk the four miles to Ted and Edna's place at Pie Creek, but with Fay in hot pursuit she had to hide out in the bush for several hours. In the end, it took her all day to get to Pie Creek and shortly after she had arrived on Ted and Edna's doorstep in a state of some distress, Ted rang to alert me to the situation.

It was agreed that Tiff would fly to England as soon as possible, the only problem being that she had no passport, Fay having burned it in a fit of pique quite some time before, just to make sure I couldn't take her back with me at the end of my visit there with Barb. While going through the formalities of getting a replacement, Tiff went to stay with Ted and Edna's son John and his girlfriend Trish down on the Gold Coast, eventually arriving in England in the summer of 1986.

Having Tiff back with me completed the picture as far as I was concerned and once all the excitement of this and the other family reunions had died down, Barb and I got on with building our new life together. For the first year or two, Barb continued to run Country Kate, the greengrocer's shop in Moreton-in-Marsh that she had bought with her ex-husband, Mick. I, meanwhile, started a small pig farm on the four acres at Great Wolford. I also went into egg production there with a couple of hundred chickens and grew vegetables that Barb sold in the shop.

Over the years since then we have run a number of local businesses between us, while at the same time moving house from Great Wolford back to Todenham, from Todenham to Stretton-on-Fosse and from Stretton to our present home on the outskirts of Shipston itself. At one time I also had a half-share in a 160-acre farm that I bought in partnership with Andrew Wrench's brother John, to whom I then rented back all of my eighty acres apart from a couple of fields on which I fattened calves. Later, I sold up there and used the money to buy the greengrocer's shop in Shipston from Madge Barnes. It was actually Madge's father to whom I had once sold field mushrooms and blackberries for pocket money when I was a kid and living with the old man on the farm at Ditchford, just one more example of things in my life coming full circle.

Barb and I ran the two shops together for a time, until she eventually sold the one in Moreton and transferred the business to Shipston. We later rented out the Shipston shop, intending to retire, but Barb soon decided she would get bored just sitting at home. So, with a partner, she took over the bakery in Shipston, which she renamed Country Kate and ran until quite recently, when it was sold on. She and her partner still own the rest of the building, which they now plan to develop as residential flats and offices.

While all this was going on, Tiff worked for me in the greengrocery and also for Barb in the Moreton shop for a year before moving on to a job with another local company. Although it was wonderful to have her back, it has to be said that it wasn't all plain sailing by any means and there were times when our relationship became a little strained.

This was perhaps hardly surprising in the circumstances. After all, she had been through a tremendous upheaval in her life. Suddenly uprooted from Australia and transported to England, where she knew nobody except Barb and I and where she had no friends her own age, she didn't find it easy to adjust at first and became quite rebellious. Always a spirited girl, she was fiercely determined to do things her own way and this inevitably led to one or two family confrontations in the early days after her arrival here.

She was still only sixteen when she first met Mark Scarrott and they have been together ever since. They married in 1992 and I became a proud grandfather the following New Year's Eve with the arrival of their son, Jamie. Three years later, granddaughter Chelsie came along. Barb then became a grandmother when Jackie and her husband Mike produced a daughter, Ellie, on December 30th, 2005.

Tiff still has Australia in her blood and hankers to go back one day. She and Mark went over for a holiday in 2001 and both liked it so much that three years later they sold their house in Moreton, along with their car and all their belongings right down to the last teaspoon, gave up their jobs, took the kids out of school and flew off, intending to make a new life for themselves Down Under. Obviously, I was sad to see them go, but I could understand why they would want to do so. There is something very attractive about the sunshine, the surf and the laid-back Aussie culture.

Unfortunately, it seems the Australian authorities are not quite as laid-back as the rest of the population out there these days and even though Tiff had retained her Australian citizenship, the fact that she was no longer resident meant that she could not automatically get the Tax File Number that she needed before she could live and work there permanently. This process was going to take at least six months and she and Mark felt that they couldn't really afford to wait around with that sort of uncertainty hanging over their heads, especially as they had the kids to think about. So, after two months they turned round and came back, bought another house in Moreton, just around the corner from where they were before, and re-settled back here. However, Tiff has now managed to acquire her Tax File Number and I wouldn't be surprised if the lure of Oz proves too strong in the end.

Sometimes, shivering on one of those typically cold, damp, raw British winter days in January or February, I think I could even be tempted myself. In 1998, fourteen years after my previous visit with Barb, I did go back for a three week holiday with Tiff, Barb's daughter, Jackie, and Jackie's partner at the time, Alan Perkins.

Tiff and I took the other two on a nostalgic tour of all our old haunts. I also made a point of visiting Toowoomba and the cemetery where Vera, Lou and Kerri are commemorated with a plaque set in the sweeping lawns. I spent some tearful moments there, reflecting sadly that there was a big part of me that will remain forever in Australia.

Back in Shipston, I occasionally bump into Roy Pool, my fellow '£10 Pom'. His stay in Oz was cut short when, sadly, his mother was diagnosed with cancer two years after we left England and he had to come back to help look after her. The last I saw or heard of him for more than twenty years was when we said our goodbyes on the station platform at Sydney in 1966 before going our separate ways – him to join the police force up in the Northern Territories, me to start my first farming job in Brisbane. We lost touch completely after that and it wasn't until some time after I returned to England for good in the mid-eighties that we arranged to meet one evening in the same pub where we had planned our trip, finally catching up on everything that had happened in the years in between.

It turned out that Roy had managed to pack all sorts of hair-raising exploits into his two years with the police force in what is one of the wildest and most remote parts of Australia. I listened in amazement as he regaled me with stories of gunfights out in the bush and violent confrontations with drunks in the Outback who thought nothing of taking on any cop who dared to get in their way. In the short time he was there, he had his arm broken by some bloke who attacked him with a big lump of timber when he went to arrest him, had a bottle smashed over his head as he was trying to sort out a pub brawl and had his nose broken in another incident. One way and another, I was quite thankful that I had been half-an-inch too short to join the police!

His police duties also included a spell as a game warden. Among other things, this involved hunting and shooting crocodiles and water buffalo, which by all accounts could be pretty alarming at times. And having become something of a Crocodile Dundee figure, Roy admits that he got so used to this rough-and-ready environment that when he came back to England it took him some time to adjust. After all the excitement of life Down Under, he found for a while that he was bored out of his skull in rural Warwickshire. He went back to working on a farm at first before going on to teach agricultural engineering at an agricultural college in Shropshire for a time. He then moved back to Shipston after landing a senior position with the Buckinghamshire County Council's Environmental Health department. And along the line, his personal life came full circle in much the same way that mine had done when he eventually got together again with the girl he had left behind when we sailed off to Oz.

Roy and I still see each other from time to time to chat and reminisce. And sifting through our respective family albums to sort out the pictures for this book sparked a great many memories. Those two fresh-faced farm boys who set sail for Australia forty years ago with such high hopes and such big dreams are, of course, much older and wiser now. And were you to catch sight of us sitting together in the bar of a Shipston pub today, you would probably never guess that you were looking at Crocodile Dundee and the Warwickshire Aborigine!